George Hunt Williamson

Other Voices

Abelard Productions, Inc.
Wilmington, DE

OTHER VOICES

Special Limited Edition
All new material © 1995 by
ABELARD PRODUCTIONS, INC.

Cover Graphics by Jim Nichols

**Composition and design:
Cross-Country Consultants
8858 E. Palm Ridge Drive
Scottsdale, AZ 85260**

Contents

George Hunt Williamson
(From the George Fox collection.)

Introduction: Ground Control to Major Tom

by Timothy Green Beckley

Ever since we as a civilization began to transmit and receive radio signals, someone—or *something* has been attempting to either "communicate" with us in unorthodox ways; has been trying to interrupt, override or intercept our everyday radio transmissions; or have done their damnest to try and have us believe they were broadcasting from some far distance place...such as the surface of another planet, or from inside a hovering flying saucer.

And whoever is trying to jam our frequencies is doing a very good job of it.

The Federal Communications Commission (FCC) has been totally unsuccessful in their numerous attempts to track down the responsible culprit or culprits, even though they have been trying to do so for the better part of half a century with some fairly sophisticated equipment at their disposal.

Sometimes these "messages" are half-way intelligent.

Other times they are nothing but seemingly "random" patterns that repeat themselves over and over again (thus indicating that there *must* be an intelligence of some kind behind them).

Sometimes the "noise" heard may be in the form of dots and dashes; or in a seemingly intelligent language

5

that no one can understand; or music may be piped to us on radio bands where no music is allowed to be transmitted from.

Often times UFOs are directly associated with these transmissions such as in the following case recently published in *Omni* magazine:

● "It was a clear, cold night in Brooklyn, New York, when ham radio operator Alex Cavallari picked up bizarre, jumping, waveforms on his scope. An hour later and some ten miles west of Newark, New Jersey, the same disturbance puzzled former Navy man and ham radio operator John Gonzalez. Gonzalez' neighbors were disrupted as well; TV reception was interrupted, homes shook as if in an earthquake, and several witnesses reported a flash of light. Gonzalez now claims he could make out a disc-shaped craft inside the light and contends the craft brushed his ham radio antenna and knocked down tree branches in his back yard..." (November, 1994, issue, "Let The Project Begin.")

In many "UFO flap" areas (locations of frequent sightings), strange transmissions have been received on radio and TV, and even picked up on the CBs of truckers and other motorists. Some witnesses have reported hearing garbled or even intelligent-sounding messages being broadcast to them; and several times "mysterious forms" have appeared on television sets that may have either been turned on or already *shut off.*

Even those with high-level military connections can no longer deny the fact that something "peculiar" is taking place for which there is no hard and fast explanation. For example:

● No less a famous individual than retired Senator Barry Goldwater—who, because of his former military status holds a Top Secret clearance—admits he has heard strange signals on his ham receiver. "These signals had a cadence or sequence that sounded like a code," he has stated.

"It wasn't like any code I'd ever heard before. The U.S. and other countries like Russia have picked up such signals (before). But nobody knows where they are coming from or what they are. I do know that NASA is doing a lot of research into this."

And well that NASA should be doing so, because on a number of occasions our astronauts have had the dubious honor of having had to cope with these unwelcomed "overlappers" as they went about their official duties and attempted to communicate with ground control operators at NASA during some technically difficult portion of their flight into space.

A Strange Story Unfolds

This book you are now holding is in many ways a very strange document in itself. It is in essence a reissued and greatly expanded version of a work originally titled *The Saucers Speak,* first published in the 1950s. The authors, George Hunt Williamson and his associate, Alfred C. Bailey, were ham radio operators who claimed contact with extraterrestrial beings who were continually broadcasting messages to them from spaceships circling in the Earth's uppermost atmosphere. At the time, these authors came under fairly heavy verbal attack as the mere idea that aliens were setting foot on our world seemed a much more remote concept than it might now be considered in this day and age. Not too surprisingly, they were often referred to in less than complimentary terms by researchers seemingly unwilling to try and duplicate such contacts with space beings on their own.

Perhaps the most interesting sidebar about this whole affair, and attempted contact with ETs, was the very fact that none other than Captain Edward J. Ruppelt (one-time head of the Air Force's UFO "Project Blue Book") once met

7

Williamson and thought that he might one day be "hailed as a twentieth-century pioneer" for his efforts in this area.

In "private papers" uncovered shortly before this book went to press, it was discovered that Captain Ruppelt was most intrigued with what Williamson and other radio operators had to say despite what would have seemed to be the bizarre nature of their claims to have contacted extraterrestrials via the air waves. Ruppelt had just returned from a flying saucer convention, held in the California desert, where he had had the opportunity to speak directly with the then rather youthful George Hunt Williamson. Ruppelt had also engaged in conversation with another figure who was emerging on the UFO scene, Robert Miller, who claimed not only physical encounters with human-like aliens, but, like Williamson, professed to have overheard the conversations of other-worldly beings on his radio whenever the opportunity presented itself.

Here now is Ruppelt's comments on his meeting with these two extraordinary individuals which should serve as further background for what you are about to read in the remainder of this book:

• • •

George Williamson, who told me about the radio contacts, said that the story started back in the summer of 1952 when he and a few other people who believed that flying saucers weren't hallucinations got together with a ham radio operator in Arizona. On the night of August 26, they were playing around with the radio receiver when they picked up a strange signal. They listened to the signal and soon found that it was international code coming in at a "fantastically fast and powerful rate" from a spaceship hovering off the Earth.

These contacts were developed further, and over a period of time voice contact was set up. All the time the

8

saucer people were giving their earth contacts bits of technical and philosophical advice. Not more than a half dozen people knew about the contacts because the group was afraid of ridicule. On one or two occasions, Williamson told me that they saw the saucer as it hovered over the radio shack.

In February 1953, the contacts stopped, but the saucer people urged Williamson and his friends to get out and spread the word to other interested hams. If the hams were "fit," the saucers would contact them.

One of these groups, of which Miller was a member, was located in Detroit. In September 1954 they picked up a strong tone signal on the 10-meter radio band. They hung onto it and soon picked up a voice which identified itself as a radio operator on a flying saucer. The voice said to keep monitoring this band, so the group did. Six people kept a 24-hour radio watch and got 12 to 13 messages in two months. One of the last messages, received on October 24, 1954, while Miller was alone in his radio shack, said to go to a certain point near Detroit, and added, "Contact imperative."

Miller could not find his buddies, so he went alone. He did leave a note for them to go to a certain place at a given time and stand by on their mobile radio. Miller went to the spot designated by the spacemen, and there was a flying saucer. He boarded it, talked to the crew, and called his buddies and talked to them on the flying saucer's radio. After a long chat with the spacemen about the spaceship and the world situation in general, the saucer returned him to Earth.

Miller claims that five people can attest to his experiences.

Now this young man has joined forces with Williamson and his crew that made the original radio contacts, and they are working to perfect their communications equipment that transmits messages on an infrared light beam. They have made one contact and tape-recorded the conversation. All during the transmission they could see the saucer and its light beam.

The crew is now set up in the desert every night, trying to make more contacts.

Personally, I guess I'm like the people who laughed at the Wright Brothers and tapped their heads when they saw the German rocket people at work—I find it difficult to believe this story. But I used every trick I'd learned during my two and a half years of Air Force saucer investigation, and I failed to find a gimmick. There was no money motive—all of those involved are scrounging for money to eat and build more equipment. Psychos—who knows? Columbus, Robert Fulton, the Wrights, and a lot of others were "nuts."

• • •

Marconi's Unexplainable Signals

Credited with being the inventor of the wireless, Marconi was perhaps the first individual to receive signals from space that did not appear to be random, but instead seemed to oscillate in an intelligent manner. Speculation at the time (the last half of the 19th century) was that Marconi had somehow managed to tap into signals being broadcast from Mars, but this theory might primarily have been due to the fact that the Red Planet was just starting to emerge as a source of wonderment to so many. It could easily have been that the signals came from somewhere else—somewhere nearer in space—but there's absolutely no way of being certain at this late date.

Canadian researcher W. Ritchie Benedict, not so long ago, came across a story that appeared in the December 30, 1899 edition of the *Ottawa Free Press*, in which Marconi's dealings with these mysterious signals was outlined in full. The story is reproduced below:

• • •

Has Marconi talked with one of the planets? Has the inventor of the wireless telegraph received a signal from the people of Mars, and are we to be placed in communication with the people of another world? These are the questions the friends of the inventor are asking themselves.

When Marconi was in this country, he went about only a little; his work kept him busy the greater part of his time, and the capitalists who control his invention took the rest of it. To a few congenial spirits who came in contact with himself and his assistants, a story was told that has since been repeated and the solution of which is not in the possession of Marconi. None of those who heard it, except the persons who insist that Spiritualism is a fact, have yet accounted for it. The story, as told by a man who is said to have it direct from the inventor, is this:

"While Marconi was at work on the wireless system and was trying to give tests to the persons in Great Britain most interested in the new discovery, he established a laboratory on the English coast where he tested instruments and made experiments.

"At that time, there was not elsewhere in the world a wireless telegraph instrument of the kind used by Marconi. There were in all perhaps a dozen instruments about the improvised lavatory. With the exception of an assistant, he was alone in the laboratory one afternoon when one of the telegraph instruments, which was attached to the coherer and ready to work, ticked. The assistant looked at the inventor and he at the assistant. They listened and in a minute they heard dots and dashes. Even to the inventor the thing was uncanny.

"No one knew his secret, yet an instrument was being influenced by some other instrument somewhere. At first the inventor and the assistant believed that the instrument was ticking off a message. They tried to make it. They had made out a few letters of the Morse code, as they thought, and then found that [what] they had taken down meant nothing. The instrument ceased to tick, and the pair had a record of a set of tickings that read as though someone unskilled in the telegrapher's business had been playing with the key.

There was no Morse code about it—of that they were certain; but they made an effort to find out if there was a code similar to the one they had received. Did it mean anything? Was it a cipher message? After the message had been passed to an expert cable operator to see if he could make anything out of it, the matter was given up as a bad joke. It was talked of, and the inventor tried to reason that somewhere some condition existed that made the coherer act as it had. Still, there was nothing satisfactory about it, and on the third day following, while the men were again in the laboratory, the instrument acted in the same way. It rattled off a lot of stuff that would have crazed an operator trying to take it. It was taken down as it came in.

"The assistant of Marconi then took a sender and began to repeat the stuff he had received. It was the most senseless lot of letters and figures. As near as can be remembered by the inventor, it was something like this: 'dgfloorx5]—'nkkxyz55n.' The assistant who was repeating the stuff, hardly had finished sending it before it was received again by the other instrument. After it came, a lot more of the same kind of stuff. For a half hour this continued. Part of the message repeated back brought a reply in the shape of a repetition and some more unintelligible stuff. After a dozen messages it ceased. Attempts to call up the unknown were of no use. The next day, more attempts were made and seemed to be highly successful.

"What was thought at the time to be a partial solution of the affair was given by a government employee, who thought the thing was a cipher from the British War Office. This was found to be untrue, and the idea that some instrument or some stray current of electricity was responsible for the freak was abandoned because of the manner in which the thing was repeated back to the laboratory."

Nowhere in the world, so far as known, is there a code which corresponds to anything like the message received and repeated by Marconi's wireless instruments. It was when this was found to be the case that some of Marconi's friends, who are prepared to believe anything, conceived the enchanting idea that it was an attempt on the part of some other world to open up communication with the Earth. They even went so far as to compare the dates on which the messages were received with the position of certain planets at the time.

Nothing has been done yet by the inventor to clear up the mystery? He is skeptical about the whole thing, except that he knows what happened. He knows that his wireless instrument worked with something. Whether it was to this or another world he was chatting, he cannot say.

"The story leaked out a bit in the neighborhood where the laboratory was situated," said the man who tells us, "through a workman hearing it. Then a Spiritualist came forward and said he had known of it, and it was an attempt on the part of a spirit to talk to the inventor. He said the spirit had something it wished to reveal, but was unable to express itself. The explanation of why it did not continue to rattle at the instrument was also ingenious, because a few days later an old skeleton was dug up near the place where the laboratory had been, and the medium insisted that it was a proof that the spirit wished Marconi to know about the skeleton."

13

The messages received by the inventor are said to be in the hands of a scientist who is trying to figure out the key to the cipher. In the stuff he received, the letter "n" is said to have been represented the most, and taking that as "e," as is done by persons who start at ciphers, the man hopes to get something out of it, providing, of course, the mysterious sender uses English and spells as they do in this country and England.

Enthusiastic and imaginative persons who have heard the story believe that Marconi has talked with one of the planets, and the only thing lacking is an understanding of the code to find out what is going on among the stars. "They believe that cable dispatches from Mars are among the possibilities and point to the improvements of the nineteenth century as an indication of the possibilities of the twentieth."

• • •

In Our Time

Though we can't say with absolute certainty how today's strange signals may be related to those heard by Marconi, it would seem that our airwaves are literally filled with that which we cannot at all explain.

During the past several decades, it has become quite common for ham radio operators around the world to receive all manner of chatter and "clutter" on a vast variety of bands. In some of these cases, Mars has repeatedly been brought up as having been the probable "source" of these transmissions—in other cases your guess would be as good as ours as to the possible planet or place of origin.

Probing the Mystery of the Unexplainable Radio Transmissions

Since the 1950s, the FCC, as well as other governmental agencies, has been checking out reports of mysterious interference over various broadcast frequencies. Whether it's a powerful TV station in England, high frequency channels reserved strictly for astronaut communication, ham sets or CB equipment, some unknown sources of intelligence have the ability to "cut in" and take over the airwaves as they see fit.

You probably read a brief wire service account of the incident in your local newspaper when it happened originally. The authorities tried to explain the "voice from outer space" as the work of a practical joker who had somehow managed to take control of an abandoned transmitter and broadcast a message from the "Asteron Galactic Command." They made it seem like the broadcast had lasted only a matter of 30 seconds or so, while in reality there were several messages, not just one, all of which lasted for a good two or three minutes apiece.

The following is a complete transcript of the "voice from outer space" as broadcast on television in the Hennington area of Southern England at 5:05 P.M. on Saturday, November 26, 1977. This is the first time the text of the broadcast has been published in its entirety in the United States:

The Incredible Message

"This is the voice of Glon, representative of the 'Asteron Galactic Command,' speaking to you. For many years you have seen us as lights in the sky. We speak to you now in peace and wisdom as we have done to your brothers and sisters all over this, your planet Earth.

"We come to warn you of the destiny of your race in your world so that you may communicate to your fellow beings the course you must take to avoid disaster which threatens your world and the beings of other worlds around you.

15

"This is in order that you may share in the great awakening as the planet passes into the New Age of Aquarius. The New Age can be a time of great evolution for your race, but only if your rulers are made aware of the evil forces that can overshadow their judgment. Be still now, and listen, for your chance may not come again for many years.

"Your scientists, governments and generals have not heeded our warnings. They have continued to experiment with the evil forces of what you call nuclear energy. Atomic bombs can destroy the Earth and the beings of your sister worlds in a moment. The wastes from atomic power systems will poison your planet for many thousands of years to come. We who have followed the path of evolution for far longer than you, have long since realized this, that atomic energy is always directed against life. It has no peaceful application. Its use and research into its use must be ceased at once, or you will all risk destruction. All weapons of evil must be removed.

"The time of conflict is now passed and the races of which you are a part may proceed to the highest planes of evolution, if you show yourselves worthy to do this. You have but a short time to learn to live together in peace and good will. Small groups all over the planet are learning this and exist to pass on the light of a new dawning, the New Age to you all. You are free to accept or reject their teachings, but only those who learn to live in peace will pass to the higher realms of spiritual evolution.

"Here then the voice of Glon—the voice of the Asteron Galactic Command speaking to you. Be aware also that there are many false prophets and guides at present operating on your world. They will suck your energy from you, the energy you call money, and will put it to evil ends, giving you worthless gross in return. Your inner divine self will protect you from this. You must learn to be

16

sensitive to the voice within that can tell you what is truth and what is confusion, chaos and untruth. Learn to listen to the voice of truth which is within you and you will lead yourself onto the path of evolution.

"This is our message to you, our dear friends. We have watched you growing for many years, just as you have watched our lights in the skies. You know now that we are here and that there are more beings on and around your Earth than your dentists care to admit. We are deeply concerned about you and your path towards the light and we will do all we can to help you. Have no fears, seek only to know yourself and live in harmony with the ways of your planet Earth.

"We are the Asteron Galactic Command. Thank you for your attention. We are now leaving the planes of your existence. May you be blessed with supreme love and truth of the cosmos."

The Unperturbed British

If there is one thing most Britishers have in common, it's their unflappability. They've lived through the blitz, survived more Channel storms than you can count, and taken every imaginable type of man or nature-spawned excess very much in stride.

That's why they felt prepared to ride out any bad news which was transmitted to them over their regularly scheduled newscasts of November 26. But in homes all over Hampshire County, and as far north as Reading in Berkshire and Witney in Oxfordshire, TV viewers got the shock of their lives and caused the usually unflappable Britons to jam the switchboards of every police station for miles around. Voices from space are not your usual evening's entertainment.

According to those who live in the area, towards the end of Southern Television's evening news program, a series of "bleeps" gradually took over the normal sound. Commented one viewer, "It was the kind of signal you get prior to a bulletin of special importance." Following the bleeps, a voice cut into the regular broadcast frequency of the TV station.

Another segment that came in was as follows:

The New Message

"We speak to the people of the planet Earth. It is of great importance that you have the understanding that we come only in love and peace. It is a time of importance in the universe that the planet Earth be involved and the consciousness of those that exist on the planet be raised to a higher degree. It is also important to you to understand that we cannot permit in the present nor in the future, any more devastation upon Earth.

"There are those civilizations that are in service to the universe that are in motion to come to your planet Earth to give mankind the benefit of their medical and technological skills, but mainly of their love. They are in service to the planet Earth and to the universe. We conveyed to Sir John Whitmore and to the Dr. Puharich that we would interfere on your radio and television communication systems to relay when the civilizations are coming close to landing on your planet.

"It is now in motion. We wish you to know that we love you. We wish for there not to be panic on Earth, for we come in peace. But it is almost important for the people of Earth to recognize that the civilizations that come, come in Brotherhood to help them. It is important now to become one with the Brotherhood of the universe. We ask that those of Earth do not attempt to prevent the civilizations that are coming, but to accept them in love as we have accepted the planet Earth in love even though it has caused devastation and in turn contaminated the universe. We are with you and we come in peace."

A Fast Reaction

According to viewer Rex Monger, "The voice seemed to suggest that the man was speaking from a spacecraft traveling within the vicinity of *Earth*. He sounded pretty fed up with the way we are running things down here."

As usually happens in such cases, a spokesman for Southern Television offered the typical debunking statements, calling the transmission "a pretty sick hoax" and likening it to the 1938 Orson Welles radio adaptation of H.G. Well's 'War of the Worlds." But as the days went on, the station was forced to admit that it had gathered no actual evidence that the transmission had indeed been a hoax. The official said, "Our engineers are trying to discover exactly what happened. We can't imagine how it was done, but it appears someone must have managed to transmit a signal directly over ours. The equipment used would need to be fairly sophisticated and expensive."

A Chilling Message

The mysterious November English transmission fits into an overall pattern of such events which have been occurring on a world-wide basis over the last several decades.

While the official stance of such government agencies as the Federal Communications Commission remains that such transmissions are a hoax, in no case has any prosecution been brought, much less a conviction obtained. This even though there are strong communications laws on the books making such transmissions a Federal offense.

Nor can debunkers explain away the fact that witnesses to the receipt of such transmissions are highly reputable people not given to fantasizing or bouts of hysteria. Included in their ranks are a number of law enforcement officers as well as several astronauts.

The transmissions have come over commercial frequencies, citizens' bands and high frequency channels reserved for communicating in outer space.

Of particular interest is the fact that while some transmissions have been in unrecognizable code and others in unintelligible language, a good many messages have been broadcast in the colloquial dialect of the area.

Alien Robot Communicates

A good example of this is provided by a tape in the possession of this author of an actual transmission received by a night guard employed by the Alamac Knitting Mills located in Lumberton, North Carolina.

To set the scene for the experience of James Ed Floyd, Alamac's night security guard, we must turn back to early April, 1975, and the area around Lumberton.

Lumberton is in the southeastern section of the state. It is flat with heavy patches of pine forests, open areas of farmland, swamps and canals. On April 5th, 1975, Lumberton became the focal point of UFO investigators when the first in a series of sightings of a V-shaped object in the sky was reported.

On the nights which followed an untold number of sightings were funneled through various police stations. Forty-eight of the actual sightings were attributed to police officers engaged in official business.

The first inkling that the UFO must have been bent on jamming radio frequencies in the Lumberton environs came when at 2:20 AM, April 3rd, Officer Jim Driver of the Roseboro (Sampson County) Police Department, alone in his patrol car, noticed a series of lights in the sky, hovering over some pecan trees. This was the third sighting of the night, but the importance of it was that Driver became the first lawman to tell of the object's interference with his radio transmission.

Said Driver, "I got out of the car at that point and could not hear any sound coming from the object. When I tried to radio headquarters my car radio became all scrambled, so I had to use my walkie-talkie instead. The light on the object swung away and lit up the pecan trees which were about 200 feet away."

As more and more sightings were made known within the next hour, Lumberton authorities immediately contacted the Center for UFO Studies, with headquarters in Evanston, Illinois. Expert investigator Lee Spiegel was dispatched to North Carolina.

Hollow Voice

As part of his ongoing probe, Spiegel interviewed Floyd. Floyd said that not only had he experienced numerous sightings of the UFO, but that he had heard a strange hollow-sounding voice over his CB radio. The voice described itself as "Robot." It indicated that it was broadcasting over South Carolina, but was heading north.

Spiegel notes that Floyd's story seemed to be corroborated by information that as the unexplained radio signal from "Robot" became stronger, other residents of the Lumberton area found their radios being jammed to such a degree that offices could no longer modulate with each other.

In his official report to the Center for UFO Studies, Spiel notes that Floyd told him that the voice which spoke with a Carolina drawl had said that it could not speak with them or be seen after dawn.

Spiegel suggested that Floyd try to record the voice on a tape cassette recorder. The plan was put into operation, and on Sunday, April 12th between 7:00 AM and 7:15, the recording was made.

Spiegel has provided the author with the tape, and

although the quality is not good, certain phrases are decipherable.

"Robot. We are clear...we may be in violation of rules. You may be violating the rules and regulations of the National Loudmouth...by modulating with this one Robot. We may be violating..."

Floyd (speaking back on the radio): "You're breaking some rules, right? Right, you are!"

Robot: "Do not modulate with this one, Robot...we are circling around and checking our difference, and they do not like for any voice to modulate with this one Robot.

"We are not black, we are not white, we are not red, we are not yellow, we are not anything...We are just one Robot, we are circling for the pleasure of our commanding vehicle. Anybody that does not like the sound RRRR-RRRRRR of this one Robot..."

After Floyd arrived at his home, the voice was still transmitting and Floyd's son typed up the following words of a CB unit in their home.

"We are not...anybody...that we did from out there... we are not a computer, but we are a Robot, we are computerized...

"We do...take the Earthling's words and twist it around and turn it against..."

Some months later, Floyd claimed he heard another broadcast by the same voice, and then the UFOs vanished from the area and the eerie-sounding voice right along with it.

A Close Encounter Set Up Via the Airwaves

David L. Dobbs says he was driving home late at night on August 12th, 1976 and was monitoring a ham call in which the operator was trying to give directions to a mobile which was lost. As Dobbs was awaiting the "repeater" on the message, the voice was suddenly cut off.

The engine of Dobb's car began to miss and his headlights started to flicker. Although the electrical system of his vehicle returned to normal within split seconds, the receiver remained silent.

"Hoping the rig was OK, I identified for autopatch and punched the access code," Dobb says. "They tell me that no one monitoring heard a thing, but instead of the dialtone, there was this indescribable voice.

"'Priority Break,' it intoned, followed by some strange call mobile 8. Usually I remember calls, but the odd quality of that voice must have distracted me. It was kind of melodious, deep and compelling, with an accent I couldn't place. I just said, 'Go break,' and kept listening. From that point on, the whole incident had a sort of dreamlike quality.

"The fascinating voice went on to say that his vehicle was disabled on old Route 84 near the quarry and requested some assistance. It was my impression that he was probably some foreign ham operating on a reciprocal license. The nationality escaped me, but as a technician I don't work the low bands, and there are a lot of new countries these days. Since my OTH was only a few miles from him, I told him to stand by and I would be there as soon as possible."

Dobbs traveled the highway to the intersection with 84, turned into the ancient road whose decrepit pavement forced him to reduce his speed to 15 or 20 miles an hour. After going some distance, the scientist found his way blocked by a fallen branch. He stopped his car and got out in order to remove the obstacle. It was then that he noticed the treetops some 200 yards away were illuminated by a flickering light. It was as if something might be burning, except that the light had a bluish tint, something like that made by the rotating flasher of a police car.

The Spaceman Approaches

"And then suddenly I saw him," Dobbs continues.

"'Him seems to fit somehow, but don't ask me why. He had come up for the car while-my back was turned and was standing near the open door. In the glare of the head-lights it was hard to see well, but he was short probably not five feet in height. He had on a silvery one-piece outfit that looked like aluminized coveralls or a wet suit. Moving out of the headlight beams and towards the car, I was about to say, 'Hi,' when my first good looked stopped me dead. He didn't have a recognizable face."

Dobbs tells how he began receiving a tremendous flow of information into his mind at a a fantastic rate."

"It was like a data link between two computers," he comments. "Ideas weren't expressed in words at all. There was just a stream of impressions."

The Cincinnati man went on for what appeared to be no more than 15 or 20 seconds. Dobbs was told he had no reason to fear his visitor and felt the figure was some sort of "biological robot." His impression was that the visitor had traveled from distant stars in this galaxy—stars which were visible only in the southern hemisphere.

Dobbs accompanied the figure to a space ship and came away with the thought that for some reason earth-lings were being evaluated by the extraterrestrials. He is also sure that the humanoid borrowed a package Dobbs was carrying at the time in order to duplicate its contents.

As Dobbs was returning to his own car at the sugges-tion of the "humanoid" who had indicated that to be close to the UFO at the moment of its take-off might prove hazardous, he became aware of the spacecraft hovering overhead. A moment later it flew off in a tremendous burst of speed.

UFO Zaps Texas Hams

Another case of interference with normal radio com-munications occurred in Calvert, Texas, during a siege by

UFOs. The small southwest community was flooded by transmissions of radio sounds with a regular cadence which might have been some alien code. The transmissions peaked in November of 1973, corresponding with the brunt of the UFO sighting wave.

Ham radio operator and television repairman Virgil Chappel notes, "Almost every night during the early part of November, heavy interference plagued amateur broadcasters in the area, preventing us from communicating with one another as we regularly do. Instead of hearing the normal messages from fellow hams, all I could pick up was a series of clicks. They were closely akin to Morse Code. Being somewhat of an expert in codes, however, I can vouch for the fact that it was decisively different from anything I had heard before. Why, even the tonal pitch of the 'noise' was odd, varying greatly from high to low. It was definitely—as far as I'm concerned—an intelligent type of signal. I don't profess to know where it came from, and I don't know who was behind it. All I can positively state is that it was eerie to listen to!"

On November 15th, 1973, the stocky Texan received an additional jolt of "Eeriness" when he ventured out into his backyard and was greeted by the sight of a series of lights. The air all around was aglow with a multitude of twinkling lights. "It was like a Christmas tree—that's about the best way I can describe the scene. All around and above me were these blinking spheres. I ran inside the house, yelled to my wife to follow me back outside and simultaneously grabbed a pair of binoculars which I thought would give me a better view of what I was certain were not airplanes, stars, or those satellites that come over every so often."

Chappel was unable to determine the actual shape of the objects but nevertheless was bedazzled by the beautiful hues of light they emitted.

25

Tampering With Our Space Program

Strange and inexplicable as the radio and television contacts between private citizens and space aliens may be, they are nowhere near as bizarre as those which have occurred between those engaged in scientific experimentation and space exploration as government representatives and possible representatives from outer space.

On November 23rd, 1977, officials at Cape Canaveral, Florida were forced to admit that they were launching an all-out probe into the origin of a mysterious series of radio signals which had forced the scrubbing of a launch of a Meteorite I satellite.

Spokesmen for the Air Force and National Aeronautics and Space Administration revealed that the unexplained radio signals had been discovered during a routine check of the rocket's electrical system.

While the investigators pressed their efforts to unravel the mystery, the 1,535 pound drum-shaped satellite, which is owned by the European Space Agency, sat on the ground and the $240 million Meteosat weather forecasting program remained stalled.

The cryptic word from Canaveral was, "The source of the signals must be determined before a new launch date can be set, because they could have an effect on the destruct system."

In jeopardy was a "World Weather Watch" experiment in which European, Japanese and American satellites were to participate.

Mysterious Voices Override
Skylab Transmission

Nor was this the first time that the space program was rattled by a so-called "space phantom." On February 19, 1974, noted syndicated columnist and muckraker Jack Anderson reported that "mysterious voices" had imperiled

26

the return to Earth of Skylab III with its crew.

According to Anderson's account Skylab's crew heard mysterious voices telling of an explosion over Moscow, an oxygen loss and a conversation with then President Nixon. Anderson considered the transmissions an elaborate hoax and noted that an all-out probe was underway towards apprehending the "perpetrator" who had violated NASA's communication frequencies. However, as in every other case of this nature, no suspect were ever rounded up nor were any formal charges ever drawn.

The facts of the incident are these:

In Rocky Mount, North Carolina, officials of Unifi, Inc., a textile firm, began having interference with a long distance call. The interference at first sounded like radio transmissions from an airliner, but later on the listeners realized they were monitoring what they thought to be a conversation between Skylab III and the Houston Space Center. It appeared the astronauts' side of the radio conversation was the only one being audited. The voices talked of a 10 megaton explosion over Soviet Russia, observed while the Spacecraft had been taking aerial reconnaissance photographs of underground Soviet missile silos. The message included the fact that the Spacecraft had been severely damaged in the encounter and only had 11 hours' oxygen supply aboard. The voices then said they were going to scramble the transmission on channels five and eight. A series of coded messages which sounded similar to Morse code ensued.

At this point, according to Anderson, the words, *"Yes, Mr. President. We understand this,"* were heard followed by a voice report that Spacelab's secret documents and equipment had been thrown overboard. The transmission ended there.

The executive employees of Unifi were not the only ones to hear the message. Anderson's associate Joe Spear found a number of others who had monitored the same dire conversations.

Said Anderson, "At NASA, officials advised us that still others around the country had reported similar phone interference.

"Now, NASA's security specialists are trying to find which 'phone freak' perpetrated the elaborate hoaxes. So far, we have learned only the 'Space Phantom' knows."

Despite Anderson's somewhat flip attitude, the fact remains that a number of years have passed since the incident and as yet, NASA has never officially admitted that it took place. Nor has the "perpetrator" been apprehended.

NASA Records Provide More Documentation

Strange sounds which cannot be explained away have long been a part of NASA operations. A careful check of the tapes of Apollo 12's log presents a vivid recounting of the monitoring of strange signals by American Astronauts Pete Conrad and Allan Bean. Conrad and Bean landed on the moon's surface and were undergoing their exercise program when the following conversation took place:

Bean: Do you hear a lot of background noises, Pete?

Conrad: Kind of static and things.

Bean: I keep hearing a whistle.

Conrad: That's what I hear: O.K.

Ten minutes later, Dick Gordon in the mother ship orbiting the moon reported the following to Houston control:

Gordon: Hey, Houston, do you hear this constant beep in the background?

CAPCOM: That's affirmative. We've heard it now for about the past 45 minutes.

Gordon: That's right, so have we. What is it?

Ground control could give no definition.

Nor has NASA been able to come up with a logical

explanation for the unintelligible foreign language transmission heard on Gordon Cooper's fourth pass over Hawaii on Faith 7 on May 15, 1963. It should be remembered that these channels on which the transmissions were heard had been reserved for space flights. And it should also be remembered that in the ensuing 28 years, NASA has never been able to identify the source of the transmissions nor the foreign language involved.

Another question which nobody connected with the government is able (or willing) to answer is—was there a secret warning embodied in the tune which for some unknown reason filled the cabin of Walter Schirra, Jr.'s Apollo 7. The melody was remarkably close to the old ballad "Fools Rush In Where Angels Fear To Tread." The one thing which is certain is that the song was neither being transmitted from the ground nor from Apollo 7 itself.

On Apollo 11, the sounds resembled those of fire engines and caused Mission Control to query, "You sure you don't have anybody else in there with you?" The question, posed on July 22nd, went unanswered by the crew.

The very next day at 1030 hours, the strange sounds began again. This time they resembled a train whistle and the labored chugging of a steam locomotive. NASA could not locate the source and made a joke of the fact by asking astronaut Buzz Aldren whether he might be exercising too violently. Instead of an answer, NASA's headphones were filled by other whistles and squawks that made auditing conversations extremely difficult.

Beaming In On Earth

There is no denying that the evidence is all around us that our airwaves are being jammed at will by something or somebody who feels the time has come to communicate with us.

While the official line from governments spokesmen remains, as it always has in the past, that such happenings are elaborately contrived hoaxes, the truth cannot be denied.

Federal law has been violated again and again. Using the most ultra-modern devices in their arsenal against piracy of the airwaves, federal officials have not been able to break one case. There have been no convictions. There have been no arrests. There aren't even any viable suspects. The same was true when George Hunt Williamson wrote about his work decades ago—it remains true to this very day!

A Few Facts About George Hunt Williamson
(as taken from a handbill from the 1950s)

George Hunt Williamson served with the Army Air Corps during World War II as Radio Director for the Army Air Force's Technical Training Command. He was a member of the AAFTTC Headquarters Staff. He received the Army Commendation Award from Brig. Gen. C.W. Lawrence for his outstanding record of service to the Air Force in Public Relations. He served as an instructor in Anthropology for the United States Armed Forces Institute, and was later appointed Lieutenant in the U.S. Infantry.

He attended Cornell College, Eastern New Mexico University, the University of Arizona, and took a special course at the University of Denver. He majored in anthropology with many courses in sociology, biology, philosophy and geology.

In 1948 he was awarded the coveted Gold Key for outstanding scientific research by the Illinois State Archaeological Society. He has spent a great deal of time doing field-work in Social Anthropology in the northern part of the United States, Mexico and Canada. He is an authority on Indian dances, music and ceremonial costuming. Several of his articles have appeared in scientific journals.

He is listed in the July, 1952 Supplement to *Who's Who In America,* and his name appears in the latest editions of *Who Knows, And What* and *Who's Who in the West.* He is included in Volume 29 of *Who's Who In America,* and also in *American Men of Science.*

Mrs. Williamson, the former Betty Jane Hettler, is a chemist and an anthropologist, holding an A.S. degree from Grand Rapids Junior College; a B.S. degree from Eastern New Mexico University; and a B.A. degree from the University of Arizona. Both are members of the American Anthropological Association, and the American Association for the Advancement of Science.

31

"Behold a fairer time is with you than any men have dreamed of; behold there is gladness again in the heavens when a host not of earth is seen of all shepherds.

"High in o pen heavens, a new Host rusheth unto you; it singeth of beauties whose eagerness greeteth you;

"There is a new trumpet and an excellent tongue to voice it; there is a new paean and a stronger throat to roll it, there is a high summoning and yet a new joy that Man perceiveth to surfeit the threats to darkened infinities.

"These things a new Host voiceth, and their silver hath a trade-stamp that rebuketh man's incredulence."

—From "The Golden Scripts."

Chapter 1
Introductory Notes
On An Exciting
Experiment

At a time when sightings of "flying saucers" and space ships were being reported from all quarters of the globe and with space travel and space stations uppermost in the minds of our leading scientists and people everywhere, there came into our hands a most remarkable document. Its authors affirm it to be a truthful report of communication with people from outer space by means of radio telegraphy and radiotelephony, supplemented at times by telepathy or extra-sensory perception, covering a period of some fourteen months duration.

We realize the extremely controversial nature of this subject and that some may scoff at the very idea that people of other worlds are attempting to communicate with us, yet we have often tried to make ourselves known to them by radar, etc. Why should not they have the same desire? According to the communications recorded in this book they do.

In presenting this book to the public we must respect

the desire of the radiotelegraph operator to remain anonymous, and have referred only to a Mr. R. a radioman, any radioman. Since these first experiments many others have been inspired to try to make radio contact with the "saucers" and people from outer space, in some cases becoming "ham" operators for that very purpose. In regard to the legality of such enterprises, it seems clear to us that since federal agencies do not recognize the existence of "saucers or outer space radio stations there could be no violation of regulations in communicating with said nonexistent stations. If federal agencies wish to control communication with our mysterious space friends, they should set aside a special short wave band suitable for communicating with them, and thus admit their existence! Anyway, there is no regulation against receiving messages from them—if you can do it !

There is such a widespread interest in the "flying saucers," space craft and space people that we are of the opinion that anything that can throw any light upon their nature, meaning and purpose should be given the widest possible publicity. The people are perplexed and are not satisfied with the usual answers. Many feel that the truth is being withheld from them. *Other Voices* supplies an answer to our many perplexities and presents a bright outlook for the future. True, there are warnings against the terrible consequences of man made disturbances, such as atomic bombs, hydrogen bombs, etc. They express great concern over these matters and for our welfare. But the messages speak for themselves !

The radio messages have been printed in capital letters for easy identification. In some cases these messages were in a code not understood by the radioman or anyone present, hence are reproduced just as received. Any resemblance to international signals or call letters is purely coincidental, and hence not to be taken as such. They appear to be a part of a two-way communication between space ships. We hope the reader will understand that, while they may mean nothing to him, they show the authors' desire to give a full and complete report.

Every attempt to present "saucer" information to the public encounters some opposition either from individuals or pressure groups. This is as true of this report of our young anthropologist and associates as it has been of all the others. However, we hold that the people are entitled to know about these matters so that they can properly evaluate them, and not be compelled to accept the dictum of those who loudly proclaim everything pertaining to the flying saucers to be either hoaxes or hallucinations. There is certainly a little fire where there is so much smoke! And this book contains some of the fire.

As time goes on more people who have had some experience with flying saucers or contact with space people will refuse to be intimidated and will reveal to the world what they have learned about these matters. Fear of ridicule has deterred many, and outright threats have prevented others from reporting their experiences. A more understanding attitude toward these people might uncover a mine of otherwise unsuspected data. Little help can be expected from official quarters because of the necessity for them to be on incontrovertible and safe ground. However it is said that the Air Force is preparing another and fuller report—from their standpoint. We hope it will throw a little more light on some of the more baffling aspects of the problem. Perhaps they too may yet establish radio contact with the "unidentifiable flying objects!" If they do, dare they tell us?

As this book goes to press the sky-watch is being intensified, radar and radiometers are being directed toward interstellar spaces beyond the visible stars in the effort to determine the source of signals coming from outer space, and astronomers are planning to have a closer look at Mars in June. Cosmic ray bombardment has increased to an alarming degree, cosmic dust clouds and changing temperature from increase of smog are now acknowledged, and space stations have emerged beyond the dream state to actual engineering projects.

The mystery of saucer propulsion will certainly be solved in the near future. Magnetic propulsion and photon propulsion are no longer regarded as unthinkable. Doubtless there exists much classified research along these lines. Thus the scientific content of the messages from "space visitors" is slowly but surely being vindicated.

Many others are now attempting radio contact and we trust some of them will succeed in establishing channels of communication thus carrying forward the pioneer trailblazing efforts of our brave little group in Arizona in establishing communication with the people of other worlds.

Were nothing more accomplished than portraying the kindly interest and friendship which the space people manifest toward us, the authors would have contributed mightily toward worldwide brotherhood and understanding which is so necessary in the dawn of the New Golden Age onsets.

FRANKLIN THOMAS, Original Publisher.
Los Angeles, Calif.

Chapter 2
The Beginning

This documentary report on communication with space craft in the earth's atmosphere covers the period from August 2, 1952 until the time of writing.

Communication was also established with several planets in our own Solar System and with space craft in our atmosphere from other Solar Systems.

For the most part, all messages were received in International Morse Code through radiotelegraphy. There was one instance where radiotelephony was employed by the space craft intelligences.

The egotistical idea that our puny earth is the "hub" of the universe should have died out with Ptolemaic or earth-center theory. If we believe in Infinity then there must be billions upon billions of earths and solar systems. It can be concluded from reason alone that other planets, many exceeding this earth in magnitude, are not vacant masses, created only to be borne along and revolve around the sun and shine just for the pleasure of men on earth. The Creator has created the Universe for no other end than that the human race may exist. Wherever there is an earth, there are men.

Science knows that there are at least 1,000,000 other planetary systems in our own Milky Way Galaxy! A lot of room for a lot of people! Spectroscopic analysis and our own misconceptions and conceit are the only factors against life on other worlds. We take intense delight in thinking of ourselves as "Lords of the Creation" and in some cases, even deny the Creator Himself. Our egotism chokes and blinds us to reality, and we deny what we know in our heart to be true. The spectroscope is inaccurate and this fact has been known and proven many times. The great observatories of our world, dedicated to scientific truth know that the other planets are inhabited by men and they know what the "flying saucers" are, too!

We are not the only ones who have been fortunate enough to make contact with the "saucer" intelligences. There are many other devoted and sincere workers throughout the world who are receiving messages by radiotelegraphy and other methods. The valuable information in their possession is almost identical with ours in every case.

These messages constitute a warning to men on the planet of the third orbit or Earth. There isn't any threat of invasion; but as a father warns a child of danger, these people who are wiser than we, are telling us we have already done untold damage to our world through the use of Atomic Energy. Perhaps it could be more accurate to say, the mis-use of that energy. The space craft intelligences know exactly what our insane experimentation has done in the past, and they know the prevailing conditions on earth at this time.

Look at the increase in tidal waves, earthquakes, volcanic eruptions, plane crashes, sea disasters, the strange world-wide weather, and the recent floods in Great Britain, Belgium and the Netherlands. We have but to look about us and we immediately know what we have done.

It is realized that many will not believe this report and will therefore reject it. But, there will be many more who will believe and who will accept its message and attempt to warn the world. We are not trying to prove anything to anyone. We have received this information from a great and noble people, and it is our duty to give it to our fellowman in truth.

Read the following account with an open mind. Think about it seriously for it is a message in a time of world unrest.

This work is dedicated to the Brotherhood of Man in answer to the desperate need of a stricken world. In profound humility we thank those who have come a great distance to aid us at this time. Those who desire and seek truth have called this work forth, and for them it was recorded.

Orthodox Science and Theology to Be Replaced in New Age

The word "orthodox" implies a standard of truth, so that conformity with it is right, and divergence from it error; but the standard itself may vary from age to age.

We can look back into history and see many examples of how orthodox views gave way to new knowledge. Most of these changes did not take place overnight. The example, well known to every school child, is the story of Columbus and how the great scientists of his day called him a crazy fanatic for believing Earth was round. This idea was not Columbus' own, for it had been circulated among the ancients for thousands of years; yet, the majority of the people in the world did not embrace this theory until only a few hundred years ago. In fact, there are still people today who believe Earth to be flat!

Many so-called prophets today are foretelling horrible destruction and doom for the people of Earth. They claim life is eternal, yet they fear the transition called "death". The space friends are here to help us, not to destroy us...and although there are going to be vast changes tak-

39

ing place from time to time on the physical, mental and spiritual planes, still only the good is to be inherited by man on this sorrowful planet!

Earthman has reached the stage in his evolution where he must be shown that he is not merely a lonely accident on one world only. His brothers and sisters exist on literally billions and billions of worlds in the Omniverse! As we come more and more under the beneficent rays of Aquarius, cosmic-ray bombardment will become more intensified and EVERYTHING on our planet will be changed vibrationally.

For centuries, Theology has battled Science, and vice versa. What they are arguing about is not known, for the two are really one, and will become one in the "Golden Dawn" approaching rapidly. All former theories will be discarded...or at least improved upon. We will know definitely where we have been inaccurate in the past and why! Truth will not contradict Truth. Therefore our Philosophy of Life will be built on a science that recognizes a Creator of the Cosmos and a Divine Plan working everywhere!

No longer will we be required to follow certain ritualistic practices or believe certain dogma in order to get into "heaven". On the other hand, we will no longer have to swing to the other side of the road to embrace the cold, bare facts of materialistic science. In short, we are about to "level off" or "get in balance".

Matters are what they are because of certain unstable or unbalanced conditions on the Earth planet. With the help of our space friends we are about to enter a "Golden Age", but it won't happen by the time you read this article. We are even now in transition, and it won't be very long before those thought to be "psychic fanatics" will find they are no longer in the minority! Call this New Age a new dispensation, a Golden Dawn or Age, a new density or dimension or Aquarius...it really doesn't matter...the important thing is...IT IS HERE!

There is another battle going on, and that is the West Coast cold-war of the "ETHERIANS" and the "MATERIAL-ISTS". Actually, there is no point of argument, just as there isn't in the eternal science-versus-religion fracas.

If you will read the theories of these researchers, I'm certain you will see no contradiction, unless it lies in the terminology of these various groups of individuals! I think it all stems from our archaic idea of what the word "ether" or "etheria" means. Upon hearing these words we immediately think of "nothingness", absence of all except thought, etc. Now we realize that space and ether are one and the same thing, and all of us, whether on Earth or some other world, are inhabitants or occupants of this medium! Vibrations here or there may be different, but all beings are "solid" when in their own environment.

As I said in previous articles and books, LET'S FORGET DIFFERENCES (which really don't exist) AND WORK TOGETHER FOR ALL MEN EVERYWHERE !

Yes, scientific and theological dogma will take a "death blow", but science itself and the belief in a Creator will go on to greater revelations in the "Golden Dawn". May our Infinite Father guide us always, and may we stand in His Light!

George Hunt Williamson

"What read we here?—The existence of a God?
Yes; and of other beings, Man above!
Native of aether! Sons of higher climes!
'Tis thus the skies
Inform us of superiors numberless,
As much in excellence above mankind,
As above earth, in magnitude, the spheres.'"

—Old Poem.

Chapter 3
Other Voices

Ancient records show beyond the shadow of a doubt that the "saucers" have been here for centuries. When radio was developed on the Earth, things began to happen.

The first report was made by the father of wireless himself, Marconi. In Sept., 1851, J. C. H. MacBeth, London manager of the Marconi Wireless Telegraph Co., arrived in New York and told astonished reporters that Marconi believed he had intercepted messages from Mars or some point in outer space. The signals, MacBeth said, had been received while Marconi was on his yacht in the Mediterranean Sea conducting atmospheric experiments with wireless. Magnetic wave lengths high in the meter band had been picked up, although the maximum length of earth-produced waves at that time was 14,000 meters. The theory that the waves were produced by electrical disturbances was disproved by the regularity of the impulses. Although the impulses apparently consisted of a code, the only signal similar to earth codes was one resembling the letter V in the Marconi code.

Marconi's experiment is interesting because he, too, received the strange V. In almost all of the radio contacts made by Mr. R the letter was frequently given.

In the following years, as radio was developed, a number of interesting discoveries were made. L. W. Chubb, director of research for the Westinghouse Electric Company, in announcing the perfection of beam radio transmission, stated that if communication with Mars was ever established, it would have to be with ultra short waves directed like a beam of light in order to penetrate the atmospheric layers above the Earth's surface. Ultrashort waves are the nearest approach of radio waves to regular light waves. The Heaviside-Kennelly Layer is about seventy miles above the surface. At double that height is the Appleton Layer. These are layers of ionized gas that reflect radio waves. The Heaviside-Kennelly Layer reflects medium waves and the Appleton Layer the short waves. Beam transmission experiments, however, were made by the Danish expert, Hals, and two Scandinavian scientists, Stormer and Peterson, and they found that certain short waves penetrate both layers and travel far out into space.

Their signal echoes arrived from three to thirty seconds after transmission. Since the velocity of radio waves is the same as light, 186,000 miles per second (now known to be faster), it was obvious that the "layers" or bodies that reflected these signals were located at from 280,000 to 2,800,000 miles from the earth. Apparently even these "layers" far out into space could be penetrated by a beamed wave approaching a regular light wave which passes through all ionized barriers.

Plans for a regular light beam signal were made by Harry Prices, director of the National Laboratory of Psychical Research in London in 1930, but the project was abandoned due to insufficient funds. The site selected was the summit of Jungfraujoch in the Bernes Oberland, 11,000 feet above sea level. Ten tons of magnesium was to be ignited in oxygen in the focus of reflectors, and the beam directed on the snowfields of the Martian pole. This colossal flare, it was believed, would certainly bring a response if there were intelligent beings on the mystery planet.

On the night of August 22, 1924, the planet Mars approached to within thirty-four and a half million miles of the Earth. Radio silence prevailed from the broadcasting stations and scientists listened for a possible message from across space. Station WOR at Newark, New Jersey, was the first listening post to report. Other stations followed. And in Washington, D. C., a photographic film record of the impulses was being made that has never been understood.

Plans for the experiment had been carefully made. Dr. David Todd, Professor Emeritus of Astronomy at Amherst College, was the organizer of the international "listening in" test. At Dr. Todd's suggestion the United States Government, through channels of diplomacy, requested that all countries with high power transmitters silence their stations for five minutes every hour from 11:50 PM, August 21st to 11:50 PM, August 23rd. C. Francis Jenkins, of Washington, D. C., had only recently invented a radio photo message continuous recording machine, and he was asked by Dr. Todd to take a record of any signals received during the experiment.

The recording device was attached to a receiving set adjusted to a wave length of 6,000 meters. Incoming signals caused flashes of light which were printed on the film by an instrument passing over its surface from side to side. The film was in the form of a roll tape, thirty feet long and six inches wide, and it was slowly unwound under the instrument and light bulb which responded to the transmitted sounds.

The Jenkins device was in operation for a period of about thirty hours during all moments of silence while Mars was closest to the Earth. Then the film was developed, and on August 27th, the astonished experimenters called in newspaper reporters. The film disclosed in black on white a fairly regular arrangement of dots and dashes along one side, but on the other side, at almost evenly spaced intervals, were curiously jumbled groups each taking the form of a crudely drawn human face. The inventor didn't think that Mars was the cause of the phenomenon, but he said, "The film shows a repetition at intervals of about a half hour of what appears to be a man's face, and it's a freak which we can't explain."

Although admitting that he was at a loss to explain its significance, Dr. Todd took a more serious view. He said, "We now have a permanent record which can be studied, and who knows until we have studied it, just what these signals may have been?" Army code experts worked on the film for some weeks without reaching any decisions, and a copy of the film was given to the radio division of the Bureau of Standards. The film is there today, and it is claimed it has never been understood.

It seems the significance of the human face is obvious, taking for granted it did come from somewhere in outer space. A crudely drawn human face would be a "calling card" of the human race anywhere !

The film had only deepened the mystery of the dots and dashes reported heard by widely separated operators of powerful stations. News dispatches of August 23rd announced that R. I. Potelle, chief engineer of Station WOR, Newark, New Jersey, between 7:30 and 10:00 PM on the preceding evening, received a series of dots and dashes that belonged neither to the Morse nor Continental codes. The signals were steadily repeated. After hours of study, the engineer decided that the word being transmitted was EUNZA. The word has no meaning in the languages of Earth.

The word EUNZA reminds us again of our radio experiments. You will note later that we received the letters EU. Is it possible that there is some connection? Is our EU

46

really just a part of EUNZA?

An attempt to contact Mars by radio was made in October, 1928, by Mansfield Robinson, a London lawyer, through the Rugby station in England. The message was sent on an 18,700 meter wave length, and it was hoped that some sort of response might be heard. A few minutes after Robinson's message went out through space, Professor A. M. Dow, the famous English scientist who was listening in, received a series of signals on his radio. He said: "It was a mysterious message, but it is hardly likely that it could have come from Mars. However, I must confess that I do not know who sent it." It was a series of dots and dashes.

Here was a group attempting radio contact with Mars, yet when they received a reply they refused to accept the obvious ! That's as stupid as deliberately going to the telephone, dialing a certain number, and when the party answers, saying to him: "I can't understand you, but you couldn't be my party anyway."

Strange things were happening amongst the amateur radio men, too. In July of 1950, Byron Goodman (W1DX), Assistant Technical Editor of *QST* (official organ of the American Radio Relay League, Inc. and the International Amateur Radio Union), wrote an article entitled, "The Loneliest Ham in the World." This article appeared in *QST*. (Volume XXXIV, No. 7).

Mr. Goodman's strange account and experience follows:

"It was a good convention, although the rains may have held down the attendance a little. At the DX meeting I mentioned how at League Headquarters we often enjoy the confidences of foreign hams who are forced to operate undercover, and how these operators in the less 'enlightened' countries really have a tough time of it. It just happens to be one of the interesting sidelights to working at the League, and I've told about it lots of times, without giving away any calls, of course.

"The wind-up banquet was over early, and I figured it was a good chance to catch up on my sleep. But just as I got to my room the phone rang, and a voice at the other end asked if he could come up and talk a little DX. Well, no matter how tired you are you don't pass up something like that, so I told him, 'Sure. Come on up.'

"I'd put my guest in his 50's, but of course you never know. He told me his call, which didn't ring any bells, and his name.

"He took his with soda, and then announced, 'Boy, I've worked more DX than anyone else in the world.'

"Oh, brother! I thought. A crackpot. I know W1FH and a few of the others, and this guy wasn't one of them."

"'I don't follow you, Mike,' I said. 'W1FH has the most confirmed, and there are a few others right on his tail. How many have you got?'

"'If you mean countries,' he said. 'I don't have any. I'm talking about real DX. I have to tell someone or I'll bust. I figure I can talk to you because you know how to keep a confidence.'

"'Oh, you can trust me,' I said, knowing I had about 40 pounds and a few years on him. And I was closer to the door. 'What do you call real DX?'

"He sipped his drink and looked straight at me. He didn't look like a nut. His eyes were clear without the glitter, and he wasn't a nervous type. 'Planets,' he said quietly. 'I've worked four of them.'

"My first reaction was to gag it and ask if he had the QSLs, but then I thought better of it. 'What makes you think I'll believe that, or even think it's funny?' I asked.

"'Look, it's early,' he replied. 'Come on out to the shack and I'll show you. The Eastern train goes out at 9 AM, and I'll bring you back before midnight. You'll get your beauty sleep.'

"I'm a sucker for any new angle, so I went. He briefed me while I watched his Buick's headlights take us through town and out the highway. 'I got interested in 5 meters when hams were debasing tubes to get on 20,' he said. 'That's a long time ago, and I hadn't had my ticket very long. There wasn't a soul around here on 5, but I didn't know enough to realize there weren't a lot of fellows on across the country. After all, QST reported activity there.'

" 'That was before my time,' I explained. 'Don't blame me.'

" 'I called CQ on Five every night every ten minutes for I don't know how long,' he continued. 'Then one night, as I turned around after my second or third CQ, I heard someone calling me. I was so shaky going back I almost pulled the key off the table. The signal signed MA1A but I never gave it a thought. It was someone I could work, and that was good enough for me. I gave him a signal report and signed over. He didn't come back! I was frantic! Here he was, the first station I'd ever raised, and I lost him! Then, fully seven or eight minutes later, I ran across his signal acknowledging my report and telling me I was very weak. He wasn't weak at all, and before we were through he had told me how to build a decent antenna, although I had a little trouble at times understanding his English. It was a screwy kind of skywire, like nothing in the books then or now. We made a schedule for the next night, and during the day I built the antenna. When schedule time came I called with a lot of confidence, but no answer. Then, after a lapse of about seven or eight minutes I heard him! This time we chewed the fat for five hours, always with the delay in his comeback. What he told me that night left me in a daze. He said he was on Mars! They had heard me calling CQ every night, and practicing the code in between, and they had managed to

49

dope out the language from what I had sent all those months. It's true I had been amusing myself by practicing the code on the air—sending a page at a time from *QST* or *Scientific American*—but I didn't see how they could figure out the whole language from that. It turned out that they hadn't, really, but after a few weeks of schedules and a lot of questions MAYA knew the language as well as I did. From the first he told me that if I mentioned this to any-one else our schedule would stop, so I didn't tell a soul."

"I kept looking for an angle. All I could figure was a big legpulling deal, so I rode along. 'When was all this?' I asked.

"'Oh, it started back in the 20's,' Mike replied. 'Since then we've moved higher in frequency, and he's told me how to build in secrecy systems so no one will ever get on to us. I can't tell you the details, but we never stay on the same frequency long enough for anyone to spot us. We swish through the 2-meter band hundreds of times an hour, but nothing would ever tag us except a TV receiver in that range.'

"'And you've been keeping this schedule ever since?' I asked.

"'That and a few more. When we first started, MA1A asked a lot of questions, and I noticed that when I told him about our aeroplanes and submarines and guns he wasn't much interested. But since the war I have to go through all the magazines and papers for any dope on jet planes and rockets and atomic energy, because he asks a lot of questions about what we're doing with them. Ever since he told me how to build a real antenna and a good station, we've had a solid circuit. He and his friends are smart ones, all right. The things they tell me always work, and it's all stuff that hasn't been in QST or even the I. R. E. Proceedings. As he helped me improve my rig, he started hooking me up with some of the other planets.'

"This is really getting thick, I thought.

"'Apparently these guys or things on Mars taught the Earth language, at least my version of it, to the other planets, and told how to get in touch with me. I figured the whole thing might be a hoax, so I read up on astronomy and darned if everything didn't check. Our skeds were made only for times the other planets were visible on this side of the world, and the delay time always checked out on the button. The toughest place to get to was Jupiter, and I finally had to raise my peak power to 200 kilowatts before I could get through, although I'd been hearing them for weeks.'

"'What do you mean, 'peak power'?' I asked. 'Are you using pulse?'

"'Sure,' Mike replied. 'It's the only way I can get through and not have tubes that would look suspicious, just in case the law ever comes around. I put that in back in 1932, when I first worked Venus. Anyway, it's part of our secrecy system.'

"'How about phone? Didn't you try it so you can hear what their voices sound like?'

"'I suggested it,' said Mike. 'But they said 'No.' Code was good enough for all they needed, they claimed. I figured they didn't want to tip me off, in case they don't have voices and would have to create artificial ones.'

"It all sounded reasonable enough, but I wasn't buying any until I saw it. Just then Mike turned off the highway onto a dirt road, and we finally ended up in a small house. In the moonlight I could see a lot of masts.

"'My antenna is made of wires strung from those poles,' Mike explained. 'I change the directivity by phasing from the shack, and I explain to the few hams who have wandered by that it's an experimental 40-meter beam. I'm never on 40, they don't hear me, and they lose interest.'

51

"Inside the shack the stuff looked real good. I didn't see anything that looked like unusual techniques, though, and I wondered out loud about the secret stuff. Mike smiled and explained that the place had to look something like a ham station—the secret gear was hidden away and I was wasting my time snooping.

"'When's our next sked?' I asked.

"'Tomorrow night,' Mike replied. 'But we can interrogate the band if you want, just in case someone's on.' He warmed up the rig a few minutes and then threw a switch. The lights dimmed a bit and I heard a few transformers groan. A pip appeared on the panoramic and Mike centered it. He sat down at the table and worked the guy on the bug. The call was MM1F but I wasn't impressed, because a lot of jokers with queer calls have sucked me in during the past decade or two, and I believe them when I get a QSL. Mike and MM1F exchanged reports and then chewed the fat about an ionosphere storm that was due, working fast break-in. MM1F could have been a ZL for all the difference it would have made in the procedure. I had to admire his fist, though—it sounded just like tape. Then it dawned on me that the whole thing was a rib! There was no delay in the comeback! Some of the local boys must have planned the whole thing to make a monkey out of the New Englander. But the op at the other end had forgotten to allow some lag time ! Pretty good, I thought, but they slipped up after all the elaborate buildup. I'll just play along.

"Mike signed off, there were no more pips on the screen, and he shut down and made a pot of coffee. We chewed about receiver sensitivity, pulse techniques, beam antennas, and the usual. I had to hand it to him—he knew all the answers. Occasionally I would get around to his rig, but he would brush me off on the tough questions with the excuse that they involved the secret stuff. On the way

52

back to the hotel it was much the same deal, but he did give me a few ideas I'm going to try. That one about compound feedback has possibilities.

"Mike made me promise I wouldn't tell a soul about his work, declined a nightcap, and then I gave him the business. 'By the way, Mike,' I asked, 'why wasn't there any delay on that planet MM1F you worked !'

"'Oh, that was no planet,' Mike replied. 'That was a mobile station, a space ship practically in our atmosphere. There are quite a few around these days, scouting the earth. Look me up when you're out this way again.' He drove off before I had a chance to tell him I had the whole thing figured.

"But have I? I just read about two airline pilots who have seen the darned things!"

There are several things about Mike's experience that tie-in with our own experiments. First of all, he said that the transmission from Mars, etc., was never "weak." The signals we received were never "weak," either. He said that the language they used was strange. Could it be they spelled phonetically as they did with us? He also said that Jupiter was the most difficult planet to contact. You will note later our own radio records, and know that we had the same experience! They wouldn't use radiotelephony with Mike, and they only used it once with us.

Yes, the "saucers" have been here for centuries, and the moment we developed our crude radio communication, they utilized that also!

Chapter 4
Williamson: His Story

It was a rainy afternoon in mid-summer on the shores of Spirit Bear Lake. This was the northern land of Minnesota, U. S. A. It had always been the same, I mused, as I stretched out on my cabin cot to read. The Redman, the Norseman, the Whiteman; they had all been captivated by the "Land of the Sky-Blue Water." Evidence is on every hand to prove that they all were acquainted with this country of mounds, mooring-stones and logging camps.

It was in 1951 and I was doing anthropological field-work amongst the Chippewa Indians. I had already accumulated many legends of these wonderful Woodland people. Woven into their age old stories of "Hairy-Faced Men," "Gee-By's" (Ghosts), and "Nanabozho," were countless tales of the "Gin Gwin" or that which shakes the Earth. These "Earth Rumblers" might also be known as "Flying Wheels" or "Flying Boats."

The venerable old Chippewa men still tell of the sacred "Little People" in a whisper. These highly intelligent little men were said to have appeared in ancient times to the people of the Chippewa Nation. While they were with the Indians they taught them better ways of living. If you ask the Indian why these wise beings are no longer seen, they will tell you, "They don't come around much any more since the white man came."

After many months of hearing and recording these legends, I still never associated them in any way with the "saucer" phenomena that was puzzling the entire world.

So, on this rainy afternoon, I began to read the pocketbook edition of Donald Keyhoe's, *The Flying Saucers Are Real.* Once started, I couldn't put it down until I had finished it. It continued to rain and I continued to read. He spoke of that day in Tucson, Arizona when thousands of people looked up to see "something" in the sky. I had been in Tucson when all of this happened and I had seen that "something" myself. Now facts began to "snap into place" in my mind. I had always believed that this Earth must certainly not be the only inhabited world in the entire universe. Why would the Creator place man, his crowning achievement on one, rather small, insignificant planet? After all, there must be many planets and solar systems in outer space. Why would any earth be created to spin around eternally void of life: to fulfill its mission as a noxious ball of poisonous gas full of methane and ammonia? I felt that other worlds were created for one purpose only—to be the abode of Man !

Yes, I could accept Keyhoe's conclusion that the "flying saucers" were interplanetary in origin. They could be from planets in our own system, or they could even be from other solar systems. And then I seemed to hear uproarious laughter, because I felt that the men of other worlds must think it humorous indeed that men of Earth on their little 'speck' believe that the entire universe was created just for them.

These men must also feel somewhat sad at the same time because such ignorance abounds.

I now collected my legends and so-called myths in a more serious manner. Where before I had not deliberately looked for "saucer" stories, I now intentionally "dug them out." At the Chippewa rice camps, the "Squaw Dances," the country grocery store and in the fishing boats, we talked "saucers"—the Redman and I.

Soon I discovered that the "saucers" existed in the tales of almost all the American Indian tribes and even in the legends of so-called primitive people all over the world! There were the "Flying Boats" of ancient India and the Orient. The "Flying Boats" and the "Havmusuvs" of the Paiutes and Navajos in the American Southwest. The "Little Wise People" of the Sioux, Mandan, Cherokee and many other tribes. The strange, almost forgotten tales of Poseid (Atlantis), Lemuria, Mu, and Pan the Lost Continents where men had the knowledge of "Flying Ships." And in the Holy Bible itself I found an obvious reference to "saucers" in the Old Testament, Book of the Prophet Ezekiel, Chapter I.

I returned to Arizona in the Spring of 1952 and decided to continue my research, hoping to find some of the answers, at least, to the age-old mystery of the "saucers" and "wheels." What were they? Where did they come from? What—if anything—was inside? What were they here for? I knew that somewhere there were answers to these and other questions. I wanted to find out.

I joined my wife in Prescott, Arizona. She had been conducting her own research in anthropology near Tucson, Arizona, and had come across many strange tales also. We then began to read everything that had ever been published on the saucer phenomena. Keyhoe, Heard, Scully, Arnold, Palmer, and others.

During the summer months the "saucers" were headlined again and again. This time they were seen over the Washington Capital and were even picked up on radarscopes.

One evening in late summer, Mr. and Mrs. Alfred C. Bailey of Winslow, Arizona came to visit with my wife and I in Prescott. I had corresponded with Al and Betty and knew them to be people interested in ancient history, philosophy, and anthropology. Al was employed by the Santa Fe Railway Company, but antiquities had always fascinated him and he made quite a hobby of it.

We discussed my research work in the Northern United States and what I had discovered while there. Inevitably, the conversation got around to "saucers." Neither the Baileys nor my wife and I were absolutely certain as to what they might be. We did know, however, that the so-called "official" statements regarding them were very absurd and only confused the entire matter. A noted South American scientist claimed they were corpuscles passing over the retina of the eye. Another said they were seeing "cotton puff balls" floating in the New Mexico skies from Texas. Others said they were "flying hubcaps," tow-targets, weather instruments, temperature inversion, etc.

We both had always believed that other worlds must be inhabited. Even most astronomers agree on that point. So, we decided that if the "saucers" were piloted by intelligent beings, they must be wiser than we. They must be, for they have developed space craft and we have not. Therefore, they would be able to understand our language by now and our code systems as well. This seems difficult for most people to understand. They ask, "But how can the 'saucerians' speak English?" Let me say it is not impossible by any means. We speak a language don't we? And we learned it as children by hearing it spoken. As we get older it is harder for us to learn a language but we can learn it, nevertheless. Are we to limit them to our own intelligence? We have already proven that they are much wiser than we. But let us say for a moment that they are only as intelligent as we are (perish the thought). They then could learn our language in about six months by merely listening to it. Anthropology can explain this fact easily.

If one goes into a foreign land and wishes to learn the language of that land, he finds someone who is bilingual to teach him. However, if no one there understands him and he doesn't understand them, he has no alternative but to listen to them day in and day out. After about six months (this varies with different individuals, of course) he will begin to know what they are talking about. Sometime later he will learn to speak the language himself. So, you see, it is not too difficult to understand how they can speak our languages or know our code systems.

If there were intelligent beings in those "saucers," they must be observing our world—listening to everything we say by monitoring our radio broadcasts.

We wondered what their purpose in coming to Earth was. We didn't think it conceivable that with countless planets in space they would desire our "beloved" Earth that we have contaminated for so many centuries. Besides, if they have been coming here for so long, why didn't they invade and conquer us when we were quite harmless with our bow and arrow playthings? Certainly they wouldn't wait until we had developed atomic weapons of war! Therefore, we knew that they had not traversed millions of miles of space for conquest.

We spent the rest of our evening together in Prescott by enjoying a fine supper in town and entertaining ourselves with certain games and parlor tricks. One amusing pastime known to many families as a diverting trick is automatic writing. We thought it would be fun to try it. We had heard that the idea was for one or two people to hold a pencil over a sheet of paper and then see if it would write some sort of a message. Although there are some who seriously consider the writing obtained in this manner to be genuine "spirit communication," we never had such thoughts in our minds. We were just doing what many people will do in their own parlor for an evening's entertainment. In truth, since our dinner, we had just about forgotten the elusive "saucers," and now were having a good time. What we did not know was that people of other worlds were watching and waiting for a sign of receptivity on the part of their brothers on Earth, standing by and ready with their superior equipment to contact any and all who sought the answer to their presence in the skies of Earth. Little did we know what we had started with our simple little amusement. It was to change our entire life!

If what we were receiving through automatic writing was true, then there would be answers to many questions. Had we, through our intense desire to know more about the "saucers," actually contacted the intelligence behind them? It didn't seem at all possible, but how could we be sure?

For centuries man on Earth had pondered the debatable question: Is there life on other worlds? If so, and this life is human, are there homes and cities where men live, love and work? We looked up into black space, pinpointed with millions of these worlds, and wondered.

Chapter 5
Bailey: His Story

During my school years, and for reasons not known or understood, I was at variance with my instructors and textbooks. I had a strong tendency to argue and disbelieve both the teachers and their many theories that they taught as "fact."

As I look back now, throughout my entire life, I can see where man-made ideas and opinions have been relegated to the back of my mind. However, it was always easy for me to accept ideas of a universal nature, and to reject or disregard effect ideas that were being taught.

Perhaps during my grade school years this unknown factor was the thing that made my life so hard. After entering high school I found it much easier to get along even if I did not completely agree with my instructors.

In 1933 I met Dr. F. E. Dewart, a chiropractor, of Peru, Indiana. Until this time my concept of chiropractic was as hazy and biased as most young people's.

Dr. Dewart explained to me in concise and simple language the theory of his profession. It was so natural and reasonable that it immediately intrigued me. From his simple explanation of how and why the human body worked I decided to study this science.

In the fall of 1933 I entered the Palmer School of Chiropractic. I did not complete the prescribed course of

60

study, but did learn enough of it to know that certain Universal Laws as taught there apply to most every phase of scientific research and to life itself.

The philosophy is based upon the understanding and the acceptance of the existence of a Universal Intelligence. It starts with that great universal principle of cause. As long as that part of their philosophy, upon which their science is based, is kept in mind, they or anyone else following a line of scientific research cannot be far wrong.

Any scientific study based on that great principle of the universe studying effects proceeding from cause instead of trying to arrive at causes by studying effects, cannot but be well based in fact instead of theory.

Even though I did not finish my chiropractic study and failed to enter practice, I am glad that I attended their school. I learned to understand the Laws of the Universe a little more. Six or seven years ago I broke with a dogmatic religion. From that time until now I have in no way felt lost but learned that no religion offered all the necessary answers to the universe. At least, none of them answered my innermost feelings.

I liked the American Southwest. It had an exceptional climate, and good employment was to be had in my field of railroading. Winslow, Arizona, is a typical railroad town. I have worked for the Santa Fe Railway Company for many years, and now serve them as a conductor.

Although I had little formal education in science, I read many books on various subjects. Several of these books spoke of the "flying saucers." Soon I began to believe that these strange sky objects might be spacecraft from other inhabited planets. The writings of many others then began to fill a gap in my mind to help me understand our universal belonging.

Many of my friends and co-workers in the past few years have been surprised by my positive statements that these "saucers" were spaceships or observation craft from larger spaceships. Since I had never placed much reliance on scientific pronouncements of the uninhabitable nature of the planets in our solar system, it seemed only proper and reasonable that they were visitors from neighboring planets.

Everything went along in this manner for several years. I was in no way a "flying saucer" fanatic. I had accepted them for what many people now know them to be.

One day last summer (1952), we received a letter from George H. Williamson, an anthropologist living in Prescott, Arizona. He knew our mutual interest and said that if we were ever in Prescott we should come to see him and his wife. This letter was ignored for almost two months. Then, one day, we decided to take the time to make the somewhat long drive through Flagstaff and Williams to the small mountain town of Prescott. We enjoyed a fine drive through some of the most beautiful scenery in the Southwest.

We found Mr. and Mrs. Williamson to be very interesting young people. We discussed the legends he had collected amongst the Indian people and we mentioned the flying saucers. We then looked over many clippings and numerous reports of this strange aerial phenomena.

After our dinner, we decided to play a few parlor games. I had heard of automatic writing but had never actually tried it or even seen it done. Since my knowledge of it was small, I had never really formed any opinion regarding it. After all, we were just performing a parlor trick. Or were we? Two people were supposed to grasp a pencil held over a sheet of paper. The moment we started our stunt, the most amazing and incredible information began to appear on the paper !

My wife Betty and I had hardly ever mentioned

"saucers" and certainly we never discussed automatic writing. At once, she was confused and somewhat upset. Before she had met the Williamsons, she thought she had married a "crazy man" because of my "weird" interests. Now she was certain she had just met two more candidates for the State Sanitarium. But she was courteous and waited. We didn't have long to wait to see proof of the reality of our contact.

As I stated, I had always believed the "saucers" to be interplanetary in origin, but like everyone else I only knew what could be found in the daily papers and magazines. After discovering that Mr. and Mrs. Williamson had found ancient legends and accounts dealing with strange sky objects in the lore of primitive people, I really sat up and began to take notice. It was most interesting to know that these people of a by-gone age had preserved knowledge of the very thing that today was causing such worldwide attention.

We realize that mature people do not take the results of parlor tricks very seriously. At first, neither did we; but the nature of the messages demanded that we investigate more thoroughly.

I feel that many ideas and impressions come to certain receptive minds that could only have their origin in that vast storehouse of all knowledge: The Universe. Perhaps many of our great discoveries came about in this way. It is the explorer in man that drives him ever onward to new knowledge of this Universe.

There are many things in this report that will not be readily acceptable to many. This is to be expected of any publication dealing with the "flying saucers." The term "saucer" itself is a laughter-provoking word. How ironic this is! The greatest happening in the history of mankind and it was ushered into the world as a joke by many.

These "saucers" that fly in our skies come to us from

that great beyond that we have not yet begun to explore. What could they teach us? We anxiously awaited their answers!

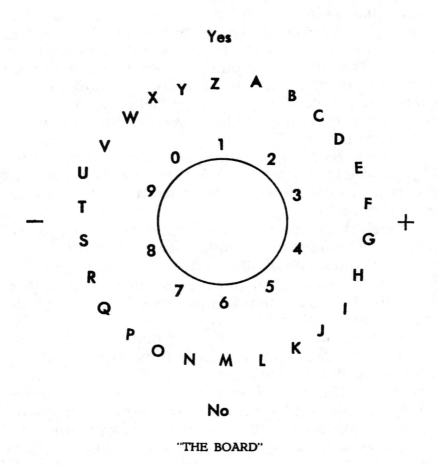

"THE BOARD"

Chapter 6
Parlor Diary

Remember that this is a Documentary Report, and truth is almost always stranger than fiction. All happenings listed herein are true and factual. Some of the methods used to make contact are certainly alien to our present ways of thinking. The Radio Diary which follows this section will be readily acceptable to many, and will give them an opportunity to make the necessary links to reality as we understand reality.

This report contains a timely message. We have decided to tell it exactly as it happened and to fictionalize none of the story. If the reader refuses to accept recent developments in the field of Parapsychology and the work of Dr. Rhine at Duke University, that is his or her privilege. But the fact that there is such a thing as Extra-Sensory Perception cannot be denied. Many well-known scientists and universities are conducting experiments in telepathy. They realize that if we probe deeper into the man nonphysical, we may eventually discover more about the fundamental nature of the human being and his place in the Universe...where he stands in relation to the entirety.

When F. A. Mesmer first brought mesmerism (now known as hypnotism) into notice in Vienna, about 1775, he was pronounced a charlatan. For many years hypnotism was considered a "magician's trick" or the work of "the devil." There are many people today who still consider it as such, but medical associations have recommended its use to physicians and dentists. And it is being used daily throughout the world by reputable men of science.

Automatic writing itself belongs to the order of mediumship known as mental, but at first sight it appears to be of the physical order. One has only to remember how difficult it is to cultivate the art of writing to realize that at all times the co-operation of the individual's own mind, although not necessarily of his consciousness, is necessary. Automatic writing has often been produced by medical men from the patient's subconsciousness; and it is reasonable to conclude that the medium's subconsciousness is operative when such writing is impelled by an outside communicator. Researchers in the psychic phenomena field have claimed that this writing can either be from the medium's subconsciousness or it can be from some disembodied entity. If this is so, then we can understand how telepathy in the form of automatic writing could be accomplished between two living beings in the same plane of existence, but located in widely separated areas. Distance, whether two miles or two million miles, would not be an important factor.

We know now that this telepathic contact can be made with human beings of outer space without the use of any device such as a pencil, etc. However, this initial contact needed something whereby those receiving the messages would not think it was the product of their own minds. They could more readily accept what was written down in front of them in black and white.

In his book, *Men of Other Planets,* Kenneth Heuer (Lecturer at Hayden Planetarium) says, "We do not know all that there is to know about the nature of the universe, and we are only beginning to learn a little about the science of the human mind or soul and its operations, powers and functions. The distance from the Earth to Mars is nothing where the transmission of the force of attraction is concerned; it is almost insignificant in the case of light, a few minutes sufficing for a wave of light to traverse those millions of miles. Experiments made in the domain of magnetism equally prove that space is nothing for the will power of a mesmerist; and one day it may be possible, through some great strides in psychology, to establish communication between two beings on two different worlds."

At different stages in the reception of the following messages, we altered our method of contact at the request of the space intelligences. As stated above, our first contact was through automatic writing using a sheet of paper and a lead pencil. The second method was employed to make it easier on us, and to speed up the transmission of words. We took a large sheet of ordinary wrapping paper and drew on it the letters of the alphabet and the numbers from 1 through 10. This still did not prove entirely satisfactory, so we made what we later called the "board." It consisted of the same letters and numbers, plus the words "Yes" and "No" and a plus sign on the right side and a minus sign on the left side. These signs indicated positive and negative.

This was much easier than holding a pencil for a long period of time. A glass tumbler was inverted and used as a "locator." It moved over the paper surface with considerable ease. Since the letters, etc., were now arranged in a circular form, the transmission was speeded up considerably. Messages received in the above manner follow:

August 2, 1952.
"Masar to Saras." (After much questioning we learned that Masar was the planet Mars and Saras was our planet

Earth. It is also interesting to note that Saras or Saros means "repetition" in the ancient Chaldean language). "By your year of 1956 there must be a new Saras. Bell Flight 9 (Crystal Bells are the "saucers") should land on Saras in 1956. Organize yourselves. There must be peace of mind. You are all for a purpose. You have a destiny. Don't fight Universal Truth!

"You are a dead civilization. We want your coopera- tion. Time is limited. I am Nah-9 of Solar X Group. I am the leader of a contact group. We were seen over Southern California last night and early today." (Sunday, Aug. 3rd, newspapers carried stories of Air Force jet fighter bases being alerted for instant pursuit of "saucer" objects. They had been seen over the Mojave Desert at 11:45 PM, Friday night, August 1st, and Saturday morning at 12:14 AM, August 2nd. Our contact had told us this information before we knew they had been observed!).

"Good and evil forces are working now. Organization is important for the salvation of your world. Contact us as soon as you can.

"There is a mass of planets in the organization. Why are your peoples unbelievers? You have begun the re- search. The time is up to you! Look up into the skies above you, don't lose contact with each other....

"We are friends of those interested, but we are not interested in those of the carnal mind. By that we mean the stupid preservation of self; disregarding the will of the Creative Spirit and His Sons.

"Your world has been observed for over 75,000 years. A survey was begun long ago of this planet Earth. How can we deny the eternal verities; Life, God, the Creator's place in the divine scheme? How can we sit by and watch the progress of evil men on this blob, the Earth? Come now, if you wish the answers that all mankind has been searching for since time began. You are wishing for these answers.

"Our group will be a duplicate of yours. We represent the people of outer space, you represent your world Saras. Cycles are computed by a group for this known as 'Timekeepers.'

"We have not wanted to interfere with men of Saras before. All men must make their progress wherever they are. But we cannot stand by and see another waste.

"We are all of the same Creation! Warning! There will soon be a destructive blast to be felt on Saras. This is of your own manufacture. Evil planetary men, who abound, will attempt contact with evil men of Saras for destruction! The good men of Saras must unite with the ben men of Universe. (ben means good). Great destruction can be caused by your H-bomb. It could all come too soon. Some destruction will come for sure! We have been alerted. We repeat, it is most important that you organize.

"Jupiter-9999, Ankar-22 speaking: Bell Flight from Jupiter joining Masar. Jupiter now leading group. Mercury, Morning Star (Venus), Andromeda-26470 and Wolf-359 are also in group. There are all he (males) in our group. You must have a group for contact. Band yourselves together.

Kadar Lacu speaking: I am head of Interplanetary Council-Circle on Master-craft. I am elected from the Universe.

"Why don't you all go eat now? We were wondering when you were going to wake up to the fact you are hungry. We have stomachs too, and we are empty. Meet you here at 8:30 tonight. Signing off."

We had eaten early and were now ready for a light lunch. The above shows that the "saucer" intelligences have a "sense of humor." This was evidenced several times during contact with them. At 8:30 PM we again received messages:

"It takes much mind power for our thoughts to reach

69

you on Saras in this manner. Again we say that you must be very well organized amongst yourselves. For better contact we suggest a powerful receiving set or radio. You should have your own set as our set is radically different. But we can reach you in this manner. Our people have trod your byways. Have you not seen us? Bell Flight-9 is a Masar flight to Saras. Masar means Mars. The name Mars has been passed down to you in legend, but it is known to us as Masar. By 1956 Bell Flight-9 will come to Saras. We have chosen you as you have chosen us and we know what your purpose is. It has been known since the very beginning. You all have a job to do for this Earth. Some chosen ones will be removed from Saras. Separate black from white (races are not meant here) and only a few will be saved. This is to preserve Earthian thought beginnings. Changes can take place, however. Yes, there will be a new Earth! There is much we must cope with. Your actions and plans will be guided by the powers of the Universe with the Creative Spirit's guidance. The evil forces of darkness will tell you that you can die for all of the research you are doing. They will say you can be destroyed, so the ben can never accomplish a plan."

At 9:40 PM we received the following:

"Ankar-22 speaking of outer space contact: You have read about the recent explosions on Masar. These were not of our doing but were caused by your atomic experimentation. This caused extreme volcanic eruptions on Masar. Our bells are "saucers." Crystal bells. Mankind must awaken or there will be an end to your civilization. More sincere ones will be added to your group as time goes on."

In December, 1951, Mr. Tsuneo Saheki, Director of the Mars Section of the Oriental Astronomical Association and Lecturer at the Municipal Planetarium in Osaka, Japan, observed strange phenomena on Mars. There was a strange bright spot on the Tithonius Lacus and a large "snowstorm" over the south polar regions. He said that the theory that it was caused by Martian volcanic eruption or fire seemed most likely. However, volcanic activity has never been reported on Mars before. But that means it has never been observed during the history of astronomical observation, which began approximately in the 17th century with the use of the telescope. Of course it was never observed before! Our experimentation has caused it to occur now for the first time due to earth's atomic explosions !

Also, a huge grayish cloud, sixty miles high and nine hundred miles in diameter, was observed on Mars in January, 1950. The only theory offered was that it was caused by an extremely violent explosion, possibly a volcano and volcanic ash cloud. Again they said that such volcanic activity was unknown in Mars' history. A worldwide observation was ordered, but no progress in understanding the phenomenon was made. It was originally observed by two Japanese scientists.

August 6, 1952.
"Zrs, my name. Transmitting. We will leave more definite information with you soon. Signing off at 9:30 PM"

August 9, 1952.
"I am Regga of Masar, Council Circle meets. You were assembled tonight. Oara is here. He is the planetary representative of Saturn. I must tell you a few things of interest. These true facts may even surprise you, but they are so. Many of your people on Earth know them to be true. Your Sun, which is our Sun also is not a hot, flaming body.

It is a cool body. One of your great astronomers believed this and stated it. The so-called solar prominences are as cool as your aurora borealis (northern lights). You do not necessarily have to have heat just because you have light. Look at your firefly. You think your Sun gives off great heat because you can "feel" it. Certain forces come from the Sun, and when they enter the earth's magnetic field this resonating field causes friction. And from friction you get heat. There are other facts about the Sun I cannot tell you now. In outer space the Sun does not appear as bright as it does to you on Earth."

August 10, 1952.
"Nah-9 here and also Zrs. Zrs is from Uranus. All planets are inhabited. Many moons are inhabited also. Planets were created to sustain the life of the human race. Your scientists are planning on going into space in rocket ships. You may get to your Moon, but not beyond that. Both of your Moons (yes, you have two; one is the 'dark moon' of Earth. You never see it because of certain conditions.) are within your own magnetic field. If you try to leave field with rocket power or atomic power you will be torn to pieces. Your first Moon is not as far away as you think. Your scientists say that the mean distance between the centers of the Earth and Moon is 238,857 miles. Distortion is present, they are wrong. Your first Moon has an atmosphere and water. Some of your scientists have observed snowstorms on the Moon. They have even seen meteors plunge through the Moon's atmosphere. There must be an atmosphere if they see them "burn up." There are even inhabitants on the Moon! We have many bases of interplanetary nature there, also."

At 12:13 PM Nah-9 again tried for a contact with us, but he claimed there was interference of some kind.

August 17, 1952, 8:25 PM
"I am Zo. I am head of a Masar contact group, but my home is Neptune. I am going to Pluto soon. Pluto is not the cold dreary world your astronomers picture it to be.

Mercury is not a hot, dry world, either. If you understood magnetism you would then see why all planets have almost the same temperatures regardless of distance from great Sun body. Sister rites are Universal rites. They are rotting. Earth is backward, too many wars. Peace to all men everywhere."

"Regga speaking. Please put water on your stove to boil. It will help our contacting you at this time."

"Zo again. 'To apples we salt, we return.' You may not understand this strange saying now but someday you will. It is from one of our old prophecy legends. Rites will save your people. We are here to warn you. If there is dissension amongst you we will not contact you. Be calm and quiet! We have only love for all men. We hold certain councils on Uranus. We must now decide what to do about your planet Earth. Your bombs will destroy Universal balance. Your Hydrogen Bomb could make an asteroid belt out of you. This happened many years ago to planet of the fifth orbit. We knew what they were doing but we didn't interfere. We cannot stand by and see another waste. After their destruction there were terrible disasters on Masar. Great volcanic eruptions took place. Many of our people perished. We would have been thrown out of the Solar System and lost if we had not quickly constructed two artificial satellites. Some of your scientists have noticed that Phobos and Deimos reflect too much light to be made of earthy substance. They are right. They are metallic in nature. They readjusted our unstable condition and saved a planet."

It is true that the ancient poets knew of the satellites of Mars before their discovery and ancient astrological works mention them. Jonathan Swift in *Gulliver's Travels,* 1726, wrote that Mars had two satellites and his complete description of them was most accurate. They were actually discovered as late as 1877 by Asaph Hall of the Naval

Observatory in Washington. How did Swift and all these other individuals know that Mars had two moons? It seems strange indeed, and one can only make guesses.

"Touka of Pluto speaking: Sister towers interfere with our contact with you. Turn on your portable radio here in kitchen. You will hear us !"

This didn't make much sense to any of us. How could we hear them on a simple portable radio? And did they mean that the new radio station at Winslow, Arizona, was interfering?

"Regga: Friday and everyday we will try radio. We wait. Try to listen for us. and get a better radio, a more powerful set. Go to see Mr. R. a radioman. He will be all right if spoken to right. Tell him the truth, that you heard that if the saucers are from space they might be contacted by the radio. It is most important that you contact us by this means. That is what we meant before when we told you to contact us as soon as possible ! Contact between 340 kc. and 400 kc. Get a telescope, if you can. It will be a sin to witness the bombs. Listen to the radio signals we are now giving to you. Bell Flight-8 is to Arizona. We eat. But go look for a radio set. We are happy. Try 400 kc. We may even talk to you! Go in your car to the railroad station. Ask there about someone who might have a radio set. Listen to us. We will be over Winslow 8-22-52, 7 miles altitude."

A staff member at Lowell Observatory, Flagstaff, Arizona reported to a friend of ours that on 8-22-52 they would focus the large telescope for terrestrial observation over Winslow, but did not say what they were looking for or why. No mention was made of the source of information that caused this observation to be made. We thought this strange, indeed. Why would they be interested in something in our skies the very night Regga had told us they would be over Winslow?

We followed our instructions and went to the railroad station. We asked the telegraph operator on duty if he knew of a "ham" operator who might co-operate with us. He gave us the name of a well-known licensed operator. We talked to him over the phone and asked him to listen on his receiver to 400 kc and see what he could hear. We waited while he went to his set. Finally he came back to the phone and said, "Some crazy guy is sending a series of V's, that's all." We thanked him for his help and co-operation and hung up. We then returned to the apartment, and when we turned on the portable kitchen radio, turned down as far as we could go, we did hear . . . _ repeated several times. One of us knew "CQ" in code so we asked them to send that over the radio if it was truly them. And sure enough, "CQ" was immediately forthcoming! This was truly amazing. We could hardly believe what was taking place. But with their superior equipment this was understandable. We decided to continue with our crude "board."

"Zo speaking: I am on Bell Flight 8 at 50 miles altitude. We promise to transmit on 340 kc. to 405 kc. with International Morse Code 8-2252 at 7 miles altitude."

We wondered if Lowell Observatory's information source was as strange as ours. And were they instructed to look at the skies on 8-22-52 as we were instructed to listen on this date?

Now we were really excited ! Was it actually true? Would we really hear men of other worlds over Mr. R's receiver? Would they answer our many questions, and what message did they have for Saras? It seemed they did not want to give too much information over the "board."

75

We now know that by establishing contact with us on radio, they knew we would accept what they said. They knew that the "board" messages did not prove their existence positively. No matter how startling the information was, they knew the materialistic phenomenon of code would go far in establishing their absolute identity. Someone had said we were in communication with "low grade spirits." And that these "spirits" were having a good time by telling us weird lies. But we knew that "spirits" would not tell us to go to a radio set, for they would be cutting off their only means of communication with us. We felt sure these "spirits" couldn't use a radio transmitter and send us messages in International Morse Code!

Other saucer research groups had suggested systems of colored lights to attract space craft. But we agreed with our newly found friends from space, that radio was by far the best method of contact. And what would it lead to? A personal face-to-face contact with men of other planets? We dared not have such high hopes, but we wondered!

Here at last would be positive proof that the "flying saucers" were interplanetary craft. It didn't seem possible that by the use of a simple parlor trick, we had contacted other intelligent Universal individuals. On August 22, 1952 the strangest and most wonderful adventure of our life began!

Chapter 7
Radio Diary

In our endeavor to establish radio contact with the "flying saucers" or other spacecraft, a radioman whom we will call Mr. R was contacted by Al. This man has had a great deal of experience in his field and holds a commercial license as well as an amateur "ham" license. Mr. R was skeptical, but quite willing to try a contact. Arrangements were at once made to listen on Friday evening, August 22, 1952.

In accordance with his request, we are not giving Mr. R's real name or his call letters in this report. It has therefore been necessary to block out his name on the affidavit also. He has recently informed us that he does not wish to correspond or otherwise become involved in the matters discussed in this book. He is, however, a very real person well known to the authors of this report.

All messages received by radiotelegraphy will be capitalized throughout this Diary. All other messages (from the "board," etc.) will be in small letters enclosed within quotation marks.

On the evening of August 22, 1952, Mr. R saw what he thought was a very small meteor display over Arizona. He also observed what appeared to be a very bright light traveling at a high altitude in the sky above him. He turned on his receiver to 400 kc., and many strange signals were heard but not identified. Al, Mr. and Mrs. R were in the R's kitchen later when they all suddenly heard strange, clear code signals coming to them. They all thought it must be coming from the radio shack in the backyard, but when they went to check, there was nothing to be heard there. After they came back to the kitchen, the mysterious code was heard again! It seemed to be coming from the very air itself!

About 2:00 AM, August 23, 1952, code signals were again received. Mr. R said it sounded as though two people were talking back and forth to each other using code. However, Mr. R said it was a code unfamiliar to him. He couldn't make any sense out of it at all. This strange code used a system of dots and dashes. After all, what else could be devised? It seemed there were more of these dots and dashes used for each letter or symbol than are used in our standard International Morse Code. Mr. R had his pencil and pad before him, and he hoped he might be able to make some sense out of the code coming over his receiver in loud, clear tones. Then he suddenly wrote down ZO, and in a few minutes, AFFA. He turned and asked Al if those words meant anything to him. At this time, the name Zo was very understandable, but the name Affa was not. Nothing else was heard of an identifiable nature.

August 23, 1952, 5:18 PM:
"Regga speaking. You made contact with us on radio yesterday. I think Lowell Observatory saw us."
"This is Zo. It wasn't altogether our fault that we didn't make a good contact last night. Affa was talking, to me last night. He helps us in many ways. Soon there will be another contact. You have already had good contact with us. Be patient! Affa is from the planet Uranus. He was listening in last night. Be careful....40 meter band is all right. We will do our best on radio contact.

"Affa of Uranus tries to keep us from talking to you. Uranus doesn't believe in too much contact with the Earth planet. Affa told me not to let you hear us, but I arranged it so you could hear something. He interfered then, but helps otherwise. He was afraid of Lowell Observatory. The "big eyes" were looking at us, and they are doing special work up there on the mountain now. They have installed certain types of electronic equipment.

"California earthquake was caused by your planet's magnetic disturbances. We must tell you about Orion. Many there wish to conquer Universe. We are here to warn you of this also. However, we find few receptive persons on Saras. You are helping us now by what you are doing.

"Nah-9 speaking: The Orion Solar Systems are much like Saras. The principles of good and evil are universal. Saras is the lowest in progression in your Solar System, but there are planets in the Creation that are above you and below you in state of progression. There is no beginning or end; no big nor small; no low nor high estate. We are all on the road to All Perfection. We must tell you that Orion is coming soon to Saras in a square star body. The year of decision is soon to come to you! We will be seen by more and more people in 1953. We want to land and you can be of help to us. Will you? We are happy. Be patient, for you were lucky you even heard us on the radio the other night. Affa is afraid Saras is too evil. You wonder how long our space flights take us. It takes only a few minutes to go from Masar to Saras. We do not fly as you think of "flying," but we drift or glide on magnetic lines of force. We need no fuel. We operate in a Resonating Electromagnetic Field just like planetary bodies do. Now we are hungry as you are. Sometimes on Neptune we eat Macas. They are similar to your cattle, but they do not have horns and they have very big ears."

79

"This is Zo. It is now 8:00 PM your time. Garr of Pluto is on Saturn. Bell Flight 9 could be sooner than 1956 to Saras. It all depends on future conditions."

"Regga: Be tactful in regards to everything you do. Remember you are dealing with Saras. We join you, it's us. Mr. R must try, try, try. Important now, perhaps only chance. We will tell you more by radio. A landing can be arranged. Our superiors must decide. Fate of all creation here depends on it."

We all wondered what our brothers from other planets looked like, and they gave us some information. However, they are usually reluctant to speak of themselves, for they feel that they are here to serve and there are many other important services to be rendered at this time.

"This is Zo again. I am 5 feet 7 inches tall, and I weigh 148 pounds. I have auburn hair. I am what you would call 25 years old. I am married.

"I have seven children. We have marriage mates from birth. But you shall see us for yourself someday! We want to give you a code so that we can locate you on radio. Please have Mr. R transmit EU. We will then transmit DA. EU equals Saras and DA equals Outer Space Contact. Mr. R knows more than he tells. He has tried to contact us for about two years now. He never succeeded, however. He tried too high and the time was not right yet. We do have a good life where we are, but wait to ask about that. One of you is interested in our musical instruments. Yes, we do have them. We call them tonas. Mr. R is fine. He is interested in us. We will be on your first Moon tonight. By the way, the craters on your Moon were not caused by meteors nor were they caused by volcanic action. They came about by vortical motion. Use radio. We must contact you. Try

80

40 meter band to transmit. Receive on 405 kc. The bands may vary at times, but keep trying. Keep listening."

"This is a member of Masar Flight speaking. Saturn Tribunal has given permission for a possible landing. Uranus has to be won over in Universal Tribunal. Saturn is the seat of justice, but not 'justice' as you know it. Orion systems want to destroy. You have more than nine planets in your Solar System. Patras is next beyond Pluto, and there are twelve all told."

"Zo again. I will be staying at base on first Moon tonight. We usually take no women on our survey or scientific trips. There are several types of space craft. One is a Scout Craft holding one or two men that appears to fly upside down and has an antenna-like projection on the bottom; another is an arrow-shaped or crescent-shaped craft, it is a Master-Craft for it will guide many crystal bells in mass flight formation; then there is the Mother-Ship that you call a cigar-shaped craft. These latter can be many miles in length and send out the green "fireballs" to explode, then photographs of the magnetic fault lines can be taken. You would be astonished if you knew what these "fireballs" really were. They are not the same as your remote-controlled devices. Most bells do not travel between planets, for they are carried within the Mother Ships. There are ships that look like tubes; craft that are round with an opening in the center; and triangular-shaped craft. Some of these ships have a high intensity field and others have a low intensity field. The flatter the form, the more intense the field of the craft. The small disks a few inches in diameter are in the "fireball" class, although they are not all used for the same purposes. Saras is like a space ship. We operate the same way. Look and listen. We know what life is. There is no death, for all life is eternal. Peoples of Saras are afraid of death. But it should be a time of rejoicing for a soul has gone on to greater pro-

81

gressions! Pray for the salvation of Creation. Goodnight, my beloved friends."

This message from Zo gave all of us a warm, friendly feeling. A stronger bond existed after this night between those above and us. We were amazed at the high intelligence of Zo. He was, indeed, a very fine young man. We knew that we no longer needed to fear these space intelligences. Although we hadn't actually feared them, we nevertheless had been aware of the unknown. What would we discover? Would it be beautiful or would it be horrible? Now we knew. On the other planets of our Solar System there was beauty. On Saras there was horror.

August 24, 1952 (11 :40 AM):
"This is Actar of Mercury speaking. We are the radio center for this Solar System because of our nearness to great Sun. We are now on your first Moon. Zo is here, also. Did you know that your blue sky of earth is due to the Resonating ElectroMagnetic Field? It is the reason your stars "twinkle" near the horizon and give off so many colors. Your scientists do not know what causes this. Some on Saras know what Chinvat is. Your scientists claim that the Solar System had its beginning in a big cloud of gas and dust. They call this the Nebular Hypothesis. Others speak of the Planetesimal Theory where the sun was supposed to have come close to another star. But they do not agree on any of these ideas. They must honestly admit that they do not know how the earth and the other planets came into being. Did you know that comets are really planets in the making? Not all comets become planets, however. Planets are made like a snowball rolling down a mountain, and they get bigger and bigger."

"Zo speaking: We can't be sure of contacts ahead of time. Listen at 405 kc.; 40 meters; EU answer back. We want to be sure of everything before we land. Look for others to help our landing. Cosmic conditions (right?) now. Uranus will agree to plans if all parties are in complete cooperation. We just had a meeting and decided. Radio contact is good, but this method (the "board") is not very satisfactory. On your regular radio there is too much of sordid life, just like Saras. (One of our wives said that she liked the soap operas on radio and the answer was, "Pooh!") Earthians don't think. That's why they are in such a mess now. Check? Patras No. 1 0-QM interfering. We will clear airwaves, wait. Back on the Moon at 12:30 PM"

Many times, the facts told us by our contacts, were later confirmed. Upon questioning, Mr. R did admit that he had become very interested in the possibility of Interstellar Communication after he read an article on this subject in "QST," one of the amateur "ham" radio magazines. He said he had attempted some sort of contact on a high frequency and a short wave length.

A friend of Mr. R., a man high up in radio circles, told him that he had also received strange signals at various times and definitely believed it to be from space intelligences. One day this friend called Mr. R and told him that Lowell Observatory did see the "saucers" on Friday, August 22, 1952. This confirmed what Zo had told us before!

On August 2, 1952, they had told us they had been seen over Southern California. The newspapers of the next day told us exactly the same thing! We learned later that a young man in Los Angeles, California, had made a personal contact with the "saucers" on the same day, August 2, 1952. The space friends were really working hard at this time. It seemed sightings were being made everywhere. Perhaps they were going all out on their "Project Saras," trying to find receptive minds.

August 25,1952 (9:25 PM):
Another attempt was made to establish a more lasting contact with our space friends. We were in the radio shack at Mr. R's. He transmitted EU so they could locate him. Almost immediately a very loud signal came in on the receiver.

"THIS AFFA. SWAP TO 450 K C."

Mr. R quickly changed from 405 kc. to the requested 450 kc. At first we did not know what he was receiving after the switch, for he suddenly jumped up from his seat, almost ran through the closed door, and dashed outside. He was very excited and called to us to come out quickly. He had climbed up on top of his "ham" shack and was scanning the sky.

We asked him what the message was. After he told us we understood the exuberance of his action. He had received: "COMING IN. COMING IN. COMING IN." Mr. R thought they meant they were coming in close to Earth, and he wanted to get a view of them if possible. We looked and looked but saw nothing. Then as we all stood on top of the shack, we heard another message coming in over the receiver. We were very quiet so Mr. R could hear the code. This time it was: "LOOK FOR A DARK SPOT IN THE SKY. LOOK FOR A DARK SPOT IN THE SKY. LOOK FOR DARK SPOT IN THE SKY." Then we all saw a strange, dark object toward the south in the Milky Way. This object stayed in that position for some time, but it was gone at the end of an hour.

While we were still outside, another message came in, but it was not as loud as the others and it faded out to such an extent, Mr. R did not receive all of it. "TO US ANOTHER TIME WHEN." The last message signed off with: "DA DA K DA."

We decided at once to try the "board." Perhaps we could obtain more information from its use.

"This is Zo. Look for us in the west. You will see a steady blue light. The dark spot in the sky was Affa. Keep trying radio. The name of my mate (wife) is Um. She is from Masar. There is a Solar System with the name Twenty-two. This is because there are 22 planets. Elala is the name of Planet 15."

We looked for the blue light in the west and did see it. It was gone in about twenty minutes.

"Regga of Masar. We wish to clear up certain things. These are things you have been wondering about. You wonder if we have advanced in medical science. We have not. We have no disease! Disease-ridden bodies are caused by man's wrong living. We are ahead of you in development. You Earth people are always thinking in terms of years. But in your years we are many thousands of years ahead of you. Venus is farther ahead yet, and the other planets even more so. We of Masar are next to you in progression. We have slight change in seasons, the other worlds have perfect weather at all times. We have great powers, but we have not destroyed each other because we have followed the Infinite Father. You have not. Yes, you have many churches and seem to worship what you call God. But you worship by word, not by deed. You say, 'Peace is for the strong.' Your Holy Book tells you, 'The meek shall inherit the earth.' 'Thou shalt not kill,' yet you kill. One came and said to you, 'Turn the other cheek.' But you do not. Your government contacted us a few years ago. They would like to know our secrets, but they never will no matter how hard they try."

The radio contact we were now receiving was the great turning point in our research. Now we knew for sure that we were in contact with men from outer space! We were practically unknown as far as the world was concerned, but they were willing to contact us because we desired to know more about them. We wanted to listen and find out if they knew the answer to what the entire world was asking: Can world peace be a reality? The ones that should have been listening were interested only in discovering the secret of "saucer" propulsion. In all publications one could only find poor reasoning and logic as one so-called "authority" would ridicule another. The government itself was very contradictory in its statements. There seemed to be much confusion in high places. As of August 25, 1952, Captain Ruppelt of Project Saucer (later known as Project Bluebook and Project Twinkle) said more competent observers than ever before have been reporting "saucers." The Captain, who started as a one man agency, now has eight full-time assistants. The Air Force is buying a hundred special cameras, which it hopes will help determine what the provocative objects are made of, and it is considering buying several photographic telescopes of a new type, costing as much as five thousand dollars apiece, with which a continuous photographic record can be made nightly of the sky over the whole hemisphere. After several years and nearly two thousand reported sightings of a serious nature, there is no discussion in Air Force circles of abandoning the pursuit of the elusive "saucers." If the "saucers" are a joke, then the Air Force had better stop paying for such expensive equipment with the taxpayers' money!

August 26, 1952:

Many of our radio messages are incomplete. This can be readily understood when one considers the great speed of transmission used by the space craft. Mr. R., although a fine radio operator, could hardly keep up with the code given. He said that there wasn't any variation in dots and dashes. In other words, it sounded as though the code was being sent over a mechanical transmitter. Also, many of the words were incorrectly spelled. On closer examination it was found that they were spelled more or less phonetically. When the coded messages would come into Mr. R's receiver, they "blocked" his set. If there happened to be a weaker code coming in from elsewhere at the same time, it was automatically ridden over. If Mr. R had turned up full volume, it would have been impossible to remain in the "ham" shack because of the intensity of the sound. Several years ago, when Mars came very close to earth, radio silence was observed every hour on the hour for five minutes, and strange code signals were received by the F.C.C. at that time. They have never been decoded and are now on record in the Bureau of Standards, Washington, D.C. It is now known that a few years ago other messages were received just as Regga had told us they were. Yet, this information has been kept from the people. Why? We dare not answer this question! Much information is labeled under that frightening word: "National Security." It seems there are those that fear that interplanetary recognition might mean extra-terrestrial allegiance. In other words, in the light of truth, the "Jig" is up!

The message received by Mr. R on this night follows. He was again listening on 405 kc.

"AM NSYKK YAM DE BEK VVK DE AFFA WWAS WWAS SAMT TK WWW AWAS VVVVV VWVV VVVV AWAS W AFFAS K AFFAS WAIT AFFAS KMS ZO ZO WAS AFFA ZO OR ANS. DE DE DE DE DE DE DE DE DE DE DF W DE DE DE WMAS DE DE DE WMAS WAIAS ANS ON 2.19 ANS 2.19."

At this point there was a pause for several minutes while the weather report and aircraft came in. Then the message continued.

"TAKE UT GEE CT DAW AIUN KATTC A UAR XY YOU
O E OZ CIAR NMOU IT R YOU WILL SEE US WH NO WIZ
NML STCNA IZ ON BETTER TIME WHEN K SHOW US
WHEN YOU ARE READY TO VENTURE C KFPS HMO. KI
KS NBZS. KKSK KKSK KKZO KRON KRON KTUF KTUF
KTZO KTZO KVDE KVDE KVQP LVE LVE TEK."

Mr. R had been listening on 405 kc. when the following message came through instructing him to "swap" to
450 kc. As soon as he did, the message continued.

"450 TE SA AFFA SWAP YOUR R 450 K SWAP T I ARE
YOU APPEAR TO YOU LATER WHEN AS OR SHIP COM-
PREHEND DA DA K SE WID26 EE WID26 Q QRA WID26."

At this point Mr. R asked them the name of their station.

"I RST 57 QRA DE WID26 QRA RRR3 BL." (End of
transmission).

"II SWWAS Y CT ZO DE ZO DE ZO K K OK II ZO
AFFAS Y II II MT WNWA II ZO ZO YANT NW YN WI.
WONT BE THERE UNTIL 1420 CMT KMC KTK RRB FLG
INW IMH. FROM MASAR: YOU WILL SEE US IN THE SUN
AT HIGH TIME TOMORROW W THIS CAN BE THE SAL-
VATION OF SARAS, IF ALL PLANS GO ACCORDING TO
OUR WILL CAN YOU. II KA KARAS IS STILL IN THE AT.
WE SHOULD BE IN YOUR AT. TOMORROW IF ALL GOES
ACCORDING TO PLAN WITH COUNCIL." On 40 meter
band Mr. R asked, "Can you give us a sign tomorrow?"

"YES YES ZO MAYBE IF YOU CAN GET A GLASS CAN
BE BY SOLAS AT HIGH TIME SEEN BY LOW. THIS TIME
CANT BE SURE DANGER TO OUR 450M COULD USE
AGAIN. THIS WILL BE YOUR LAST CONTACT UNTIL SAT-
URDAY WHEN YOU WILL HAVE TWO VISITORS FROM
OUTSIDE."

This was a message from Mars! We had thought radio communication with spacecraft possible, but direct contact with another planet never! Of course, our messages were probably relayed to Mars by the space craft using their superior equipment. Surely the people of outer space were interested in every man, woman and child on earth.

Evidently they meant for us to obtain a telescope and look at the sun at noon. And did they mean that Lowell Observatory was watching? They had told us the sun was a cool body so we could understand what they meant. Mr. R was amazed and very excited. What had they meant by, "You will have two visitors from outside?" For a moment he thought it was possible two people from outer space were going to pay him a visit. He turned to Al questioningly and said, "Are you expecting any company Saturday?" Al told him that Mr. and Mrs. Williamson were coming to Winslow from Prescott for the week-end. How did Mars receive this information? We wondered!

The above radio message is of great interest when considering what happened on Wednesday following, August 27, 1952.

The evening newscasts carried the following story. At 12:00 noon a large fleet of aluminum-colored "saucers" were sighted over Yuma, Arizona. Also, over Yuma at the same time, a jet fighter pilot and his jet plane crashed to the ground. The cause of the accident was claimed to be unknown!

August 28, 1952.

The *Los Angeles Times* carried a very interesting article on this date. The astronomers at Mt. Wilson Observatory had observed strange, gigantic sun-spots on the sun around noon, August 27, 1952. The report stated that these spots were extremely large and that this was a very rare happening as it was now a period of declining sunspot activity! Instead of these spots lasting the usual period, they were gone the very next day!

Was this the "sign" they had promised us for High Time? We knew that many observatories were doing considerable research on this "saucer" problem. The 200-inch Hale telescope on Mt. Palomar, California, was supposed to be probing the vastness of the outer universe. Yet, in October, 1952 they spent their time at Mt. Palomar looking over the Moon, Jupiter, Saturn, Mars, and other bodies of our own Solar System. Why all the sudden interest in the neighboring planets? Was it all to discover some outpost of the space intelligences? We wonder, yet we know that all this great telescope has discovered has not been made public.

The evening of August 28, 1952 was spent in taking a drive from Winslow to Prescott to visit Mr. and Mrs. Williamson. We saw eight or nine objects in the southwest sky. They seemed to be traveling at a high rate of speed in a "V" formation.

At 11:30 PM in Prescott, Arizona, we again made contacts by the "board."

"Regga speaking: The sun-spots were a sign to you. We help. The plane at Yuma was an accident, we did not shoot him down. The jet got too near our magnetic field. He saw us. Be patient with Affa, he hasn't learned English well. He is fine. We will do our best. Be careful. All is up to you. We travel speed of light at times. Your scientists say it is 186,000 miles per second. That is correct in some cases, but it is not constant, it varies. Our ships operate on east-west and north-south force lines."

"This is Zo. Our worlds have the same atmosphere as yours. Some men of Saras will make visits someday to our worlds. There are certain men trying hard to contact us, but we will not pay any attention to them. Mr. R was skeptical at first. Remember, Orion is evil. The movie, *The Day the Earth Stood Still* was for a purpose and was more fact than fiction. Watch all nature for signs of catastrophe. These signs, such as tornados, earthquakes, floods, and so on will come to Saras soon and will get worse as time goes on. U.S.S.R. is aware of us, too. Earth's last mile, we sad. It is impossible to reason with the peoples of Earth. Soon all could end here. Some will not see it, except from else-where, from outside." August 30, 1952 (12:55 PM):

During our radio contacts there were usually eight or nine witnesses present in Mr. R's "ham" shack. Those listed on the affidavit are: Mr. R; Mrs. R; Betty Bowen, student; Ronald Tucker, student; George H. Williamson, anthropologist; Mrs. Betty J. Williamson; Mr. Alfred C. Bailey, Santa Fe Railroad conductor; Mrs. Betty M. Bailey. Others present at various times were relatives and friends. Al's mother, Mrs. Geraldine Bailey of Los Angeles, California was present on several occasions. She has followed a very dogmatic religion all of her life, yet the very nature of the radio contacts opened her eyes to much truth of a Universal nature. She is now completely convinced of the authenticity of our contacts by radiotelegraphy.

Mr. R thought there existed the possibility that a hoax was being perpetrated on him. He was now certain of the sincerity of all of us, but perhaps some other "ham" had been sending the "space" messages. He has a very calculating, scientific type of mind and he wanted to be sure. If it was true he wanted to continue on with it. If it was a hoax he wanted it to end and quickly. We felt his skepticism was somewhat justifiable. After all, truth will stand any test.

One night, in the radio shack, Mr. R decided to try a test. He told none of the witnesses present what he was going to do, not even his own wife. In fact, he told us all about a week after the happening. He wanted plenty of

91

time to think it over. This test was of such a nature, that if the messages were a hoax, they would have been revealed as such immediately. He was seated at his radio set, with his back to all those present. He had sent a question over his transmitter on the 40 meter band and he received an answer. Without any warning he quickly switched to 160 meters and asked another question. To his surprise, an answer was soon forthcoming! Any radioman knows that no power on earth would have enabled any operator to know where he was switching to! Even if Mr. R had told the other operator that he was going to switch to 160 meters, still they would not have found him on that band until after the question had been asked. And, of course, they couldn't have answered the question if they hadn't heard it! An operator cannot make such a switch without telling what he is going to do and then giving plenty of time for the other side to find him on the new band.

The space intelligences really passed this simple, but very exacting test. This proved one of two things: Perhaps the space friends were using telepathy. Why not? If they were far ahead of us in development they possibly have acquired proficiency in ExtraSensory Perception. It is also possible that their superior equipment allows them to receive no matter what band is used in communicating with them. It really matters little how it was accomplished. The important thing is that it was done! This was undeniable proof to Mr. R. He no longer had any doubts in his mind; he wanted to learn more.

"This is Zo speaking. We might even talk over radio to you soon. Use radio tonight on 450 kc. or 405 kc. All on Moon. Council meets. Interested researchers represent Saras, as you do."

"Affa is here. Oarhae retto! We speak the original language. We call it the Mother or Solar Tongue. The Solex Mal. Peoples of Saras spoke this Universal language long ago. Your Holy Book tells you the story of this. Your linguists will tell you that all languages appear to come from a common language. They do not know what this language is, however. It is closely related to the most ancient languages on Saras and ante-dated them. It is a symbolical pictographic language. All men of other worlds speak this language. You are a divided people, and you speak many tongues."

"This is Kadar Lacu. I am head of the Universal Tribunal. I am now on the Planet Hatonn in Andromeda."

"Regga speaking. We will try hard to see you soon. Greetings to Mr. R. Try 405 kc. and 450 kc. Our sets are quite different, but we contact you. Your government knows who we are."

We had planned a radio contact for the night of August 30, 1952, as Mr. and Mrs. Williamson were present as the radio contact had said they would be. We believe failure resulted because of the unexpected visitor who came to the "ham" shack. There was a great deal of confusion, as we tried to explain to him the nature of what we had been receiving. He was the type of person who refuses to believe in "saucers" or extra-terrestrial people. If one landed in front of him, he would explain it away. Anyway, the radio was silent this night.

August 31, 1952.

"This is Zo. Try not to be unattentive tonight, please. Concentrate. Send EU often over radio so we can locate you on beams of ionized particles. We can direct a beam straight to your antenna. We can locate you from ends of Omniverse."

• • •

"Actar speaking. Certain great powers in your world wish to see us go away or see us destroyed. Neither will happen. These powers fear us, and when you fear any-

93

thing you hate it. All planets have come to help certain ones on Saras. Those of the right mind are one with us! We will not harm anyone, only their own thoughts can do that. Evil destroys evil. Bounce back! Certain seeds have been placed on Saras. To the apples we salt, we return."

• • •

"Kadar Lacu, my brothers. I am several hundred years old. A mere youth. The time has come to reveal these things to you. If man would only realize that he should love his brother."

• • •

"Be at attention. I am Ponnar, a Universal Head. I am on Hatonn."

• • •

"This is Sedat speaking. I am the Universal Record Keeper. Your records and those of many others are here on Hatonn in the Temple of Records. The planet known as Elala was once called Wogog."

"Ponnar again, we are very strong now. Magritonic waves at pitch of 999887 and micomitronie vibrations can tear a radio receiver to pieces if not used correctly. Mr. R wonders why we have not contacted well-known scientists. We have contacted them, but many will not listen. They think Universal laws are insane! Garr of Pluto is here, also Oara of Saturn and Zo, he is on Moon. More detonations soon, more disasters on Saras. Quickly, not too much time left. Worlds can end. Many. scientists will refuse to continue work on bombs!"

• • •

Although we tried desperately for radio contact this

night, we received nothing. One very loud signal came in about 9:10 PM and completely "blocked" Mr. R's set. It lasted for about 15 seconds. It is possible it was spacecraft, but nothing of value was learned from it.

A strange reddish light, like a fireball, flashed across the northern Arizona skies about 9:28 PM. It was viewed in Albuquerque, New Mexico; Kingman, Arizona; and Prescott, Arizona. In Albuquerque, the fireball appeared bluish-green. The C. A. A. reported it had received radio reports of the strange object from planes in the air at the time.

September 1, 1952 (12:45 PM):
"Kadar Lacu. Too many people last night. Much confusion. Fewer the better for mind concentration. Otherwise conflicting thoughts. We have not traveled all the way to Saras to give misinformation. Many receptive people of Saras have been living with those who are doltish for too long. Seeds may be planted but they can rot and never reach maturity."

• • •

"Ponnar speaking. Do not think of us as gods. We are men like yourselves. We are only far ahead of you in progression. What we are today you can be tomorrow. The Creative Spirit is greater than man. At mention of His name, all worlds should bow. Do not speak of Him lightly. When it is safe we shall come in on radio. If you knew how soon destruction could come to Saras you would go screaming through the streets! We have saved your world several times already. The United Nations would believe certain men, if catastrophes were foretold before they happened. Maybe certain men will be raised up for this duty. It is later than you think! You must at all times try to be in harmony with each other. Love one another, my friends."

September 3, 1952 (8:23 PM):

"Ponnar speaking. There are now many young people in your world who understand our message. They will accept it quickly for they are of the New Age. The Great Awakening is here. Many of our people are in your world now, and many people of Saras have been taken to outer space through the years. There is a young man in Ohio you must contact. He is of the right mind and heart. Many will not believe, but there are many who have received information as you have, and they will be joyous to know of your work. The so-called "meteor" seen Sunday over your area was us. It was a ball-globe being on its duty. We will be seen in the skies often. But do not strain to see us. When it is right for you to view us, you will. Our love to you all."

September 11, 1952 (5:30 PM):

"This is Zo. We will soon be at our meeting place on Fowser, the 'dark' moon of your Earth. You are wondering about the Cosmic Dust cloud that you have heard shall soon come to Saras. Yes, this is true. It will come. And it will darken the sun and moon. Strange things will happen in your world. Great meteors shall be seen in the skies. I hope we might have a landing soon. Try radio again soon. U.S.S.R. has been doing research in magnetic science. Recently many scientists were destroyed in Baltic area, when a terrific explosion took place there. You will always notice a drop in temperature after these explosions. Oara of Saturn is here. You must know that Saras is a Masar name for your planet. Others call your world Chan. (Chan is very similar to certain ancient words meaning, "afflicted"). If we can arrange a landing, do not fear impostors. You can be sure it will be us. On Hatonn your records can be seen. All thoughts are recorded there. Crystals are valuable to us. With a crystal miracles can be performed.

Don't forget that there are evil forces. They will try to break you up, but stay together now, for the time is close. Do not get sidetracked. End soon, time short."

At 9:00 PM we received a wonderful message from the Saturn Tribunal. It humbled us and made us realize that it was very necessary for us to be of one mind.

"Zo again. As time goes by, the way will be made harder and harder to make contact with us, for evil will be pushed closer and closer to Saras. Therefore, we must make landing contact soon. Be very careful. You may go your own way if you wish, but you know what we have told you. If you believe us you will act accordingly. What you do with this knowledge is up to you. What we have told you will all come to pass. No man knows the hour, but it will come. Others have been told, but they went the way of all flesh on Saras. That's why we have been around for so long. Evil forces are always strong. Human nature has always fought this forbidden knowledge. Forces play on human frailties. Many have known in centuries past, but they either go insane because they couldn't live Universal Law or because they couldn't meet change. All changes but change itself. Few have been receptive, but you have been. Therefore, we have been interested in you. You know what must be done, so do it. We will do our part if you do yours. If there is disharmony amongst you, we are confused and cannot make definite plans. We must know what you intend to do. We told you over the radio to show us when you are ready to venture. The blind of Saras are more blind now. People cannot see the handwriting on the wall." "Ponnar. Look to Him for strength in this hour of universal doom. Without Him, all is lost. The Creative Spirit watches."

97

"Kadar Lacu speaking. Do you realize what is at hand? Are our signs to you not enough? Every step you take is a part of a plan to further progress. Has not everything we told you come true?"

"Zo, my brothers. We happy to know all of you, but we are sad now. We hope you feel in heart as we do. We have told you that if it is possible for us to impress you, then evil forces can impress you too. Certainly you aren't compelled to do as we say to do. But we must co-operate with each other. All must help. If there is one mind out of tune, all is lost. We didn't intend for you to stay up nights. After all, you are adults now and must regulate your own daily schedule. There is work to be done, but when it is done is your own individual problem. Right? Check? We wait. We cannot fight opposition. After all, that's the trouble with Saras now. Men cannot get together and love each other. We are humble; want you to be humble too."

"I am Suttku, Judge of Saturn Council. We know what is in your minds."

● ● ●

"This is Wan-4 of the Safanian Solar System speaking. We are pledged to those of receptive minds for all time past. But you can break the bonds tying us together if you will it. It is your choice, my friends."

"Regga. You must decide now. Council waits. Worlds hang in balance. We can't wait much longer. Our time is short. If some of us must be sacrificed, then His will be done. We have come to Saras over millions of miles at a terrible cost. This has been because of our love for all men, everywhere. We are here to help those who wish to be helped. You have done nothing to displease us. But certain forces will try to discourage you in this undertaking that lies just ahead of you. Remember that weeks ago we told you to organize, be careful, and to be of one mind. The Universe awaits. Do you understand? We cannot do anything but good. Law of Universe. If we do anything but good, then we are evil. You want to do good, we know that."

• • •

"This is Adu of Hatonn. You are given impressions on what to do. There are those on Saras who contact us this way. But you haven't learned to separate your own thoughts from ours. Action speaks louder than words. That is an old Saras saying. We act, you act. Push-pull. Do whatever you think is right and necessary. We will guide you with the help of the Infinite Father."

• • •

"Zo. We will not tell you what to do. Up to you. Council waits. What are you going to do? Plan.

"We must know. Then decide your steps. Be positive now. We can land soon. Certain conditions are necessary. You know what. Our regards to you. We cry, we are sad....No one will listen to us!"

• • •

"Ponnar. We help you. All will be lost on Saras. All men's dreams and ambitions gone in a second. We are trying to help, that is why we are here. Uranus is still unsure. We go. Look for us later tonight. Go now to first Moon. Salutes! Goodnight, my friends."

September 15, 1952 (9:30 PM):
On September 13 and 14, 1952, loud, strong signals

99

were picked up by Mr. R. However, no code came in.

"Ponnar speaking. The Cosmic Dust Storm is true, I confirm its coming to Saras."

September 19, 1952 (6 :30 PM):
"Zo again. Ro from the Toresoton Solar System is here with me and wishes to greet you. We walk the streets, but cannot come to visit with you in your home just yet. We cannot say why. We have friends on Elala, Planet 15 in Solar System 22. The Four Great Primary Forces are: Static Magnetic Field; Electro-Static Field; ElectroMagnetic Wave; Resonating ElectroMagnetic Field. Your scientists do not understand the last one mentioned. We have a symbol for this in the Solex Mal. It is similar to your so-called swastika. The Four Forces coming out of the Creator. It is one of the most ancient of Saras symbols. That is not strange. It is because the ancient people of your world understood nature and this knowledge has since been lost to you."

September 20, 1952 (8 :30 PM):
"This is Zo. We can hear you no matter what meter band you send on. We have heard all the messages you have sent to us by radio transmitter and more. We have impressed you from time to time, and will continue to do so. Now what I am going to tell you is going to seem foolish. It is the way we do things at times. This is so it will all appear in a most conventional manner. You were impressed to go and see a certain motion picture. You did not know that the cartoon was Bugs Bunny in "The Hasty Hare." We mentioned Bugs Bunny to you several times before, but you thought it was foolish and didn't enter it into your records. We had our reasons. This cartoon was about a "flying saucer" and its coming to earth. You saw

the letter held in the hand of the saucer pilot and you noticed that its date was 9-27. This date is important in 1952. You will see!"

• • •

"Actar of Mercury speaking. Mr. R is to transmit EU EU WE ARE READY TO VENTURE. Then we will answer. We will tell you whatever is necessary over your receiver."

• • •

Since our space friends talked of a landing so often, we decided to have a picnic in the mountains and perhaps they would land for us. This way we could relax, away from the activity of town, and enjoy a fine week-end. If September 27th was important, we wanted to be in on it. Mr. and Mrs. Williamson arrived in Winslow on September 26th.

September 27, 1952 (12:10 PM):
"Zo speaking. Try tomorrow for a landing as planned. Worlds can be saved. There is a meeting on Pluto. Kadar Lacu is there. Mr. R must try radio often. This contact must be a success."

• • •

"Wan-4. Some of us are from distant systems. Oara, Actar, Ro, and Nah-9 send their greetings to you."

• • •

"Suttku. We are assembling on Moon now. Danger to you as landing becomes a reality. Landing area you picked is not perfect, but good. We will circle area for several minutes first. We usually do this. We are feeling good over this, my friends."

• • •

"Kadar Lacu again. Actar is with Nah-9 of Solar X Group in the ship, 'Trocton.' I am on Pluto. Masar will be in your atmosphere tonight. Try for radio contact for sure. Love."

"Zo. Plan well to avoid slipups. Follow our instructions or we can't come in. Some will try to trick us. Must be careful. Mr. R must try to be calm while at radio. He wants contact very much. Too much concentration is a block. We will protect the group. My wife, Um, is the first woman in her position to come into your atmosphere. She comes to help the women of group. Prepare yourselves quickly now. There must be harmony. Try hard. Do the best you can."

"This is Lomec of Venus. I am with Terra on Ship-Xi9 coming in to Saras. You will be contacted tonight by radio. Greetings to all."

• • •

We had a short rest and continued our contact at 5:30 PM

"Zo. Many are here and greet you. Kadar Lacu had a meeting on Pluto with Touka. We are now several miles above you. 2:00 PM is all right for landing tomorrow. Be sure to try radio tonight. There must be no confusion. Watch. Worlds wait. My young son, Elex, greets you all. He is with me now. If you only knew what you did to your body by smoking you would quit at once! We never use tobacco. It is poison. Bell Flight of 200 craft from Safanian Solar System; 500 from the Toresoton Solar System. There are 14,000 bells near the second Moon, Fowser. We have many bells in our mothercraft."

102

It was 5:30 PM when they told us they were over Winslow. At 5:55 PM we heard a tremendous swishing sound and a roar. The neighbors heard it also and couldn't figure out what it was. It was definitely not a jet plane. It was a sound that we couldn't recognize. It was more like the sound of a big beehive. After we went outside we saw them in the distance moving at great speed through the sky.

• • •

"Actar speaking. Try 405 kc. tonight. Ronem."

• • •

"This is Um, wife of Zo. I have my own ship called, 'Belga.' Women do not ride with men on journeys to Saras because of the nature of such trips. My love to each and every one of you."

"I am Noro, my brothers. Head of landing contact group. Here are instructions for you. Ship of Planet Masar will attempt landing Saras tomorrow at 2:00 PM. Ship of Regga with Zo. Its name is 'Clacteem.' Many Crystal Bells over your world tonight."

"Kadar Lacu speaking. I designed the ship 'Clacteem.' It is a special landing craft. We will have much to tell you when we see you. Our form will touch your form. It is the Father's plan. Mr. R may not wish to go. He is needed on Saras for a purpose. All of this is up to you. Whatever you wish to do."

• • •

"This is Zago of Contact Group. When we land we shall say to you in the Solex Mal: Tu Vec Saturn Do Pattla Barraga.' Then you will answer us by saying, 'Udum Regan

103

Vec Yonto Nictum Barraga.' Vec means space. Barraga means friends."

• • •

"Kadar Lacu again. Landing ship is being readied on Fowser. Big observatories of world look at Moon and see many craft there. They know they are not seeing locusts. Radio tonight."

• • •

"Ponnar speaking. Soon I shall have beautiful words to say to you."

In the evening we were at Mr. R's in the "ham" shack. We all felt that we would have a contact with our space friends, for they always told us the truth. Eight people were present besides Mr. R's father-in-law from Tennessee. He had arrived almost unexpectedly. The results of the radio contacts were astounding. We never dreamed that we would have such experiences. When the set was turned on we had almost immediate contact.

• • •

"AGFA AFFA SARAS IS LISTING 92% TO—.
HERE IS THE PLANET OF SAGAFARIS CALLING SARAS. THIS IS THE PLANET OF SAGAFARIS CALLING SARAS. AGFA. VERY POOR CONDITION EXISTS. WS VENIS VENIS. TFAS KS AR RAGIF KONT VA."

When Mr. R received the message that the planet Earth was listing 92%, he turned to us and said, "I can't go for that." However, it is obvious that they were not refer-ring to our method of dividing a circle. The word Sagafaris was repeated several times each time it came in. By "very poor condition exists," they were referring to Earth.

• • •

"SARAS PLESE SARAS PLESE V V VARY 92 HASTE."

Mr. R quickly turned to 92 meters on the receiver. This band is used for aircraft communication. It seemed a speech was being given in a large auditorium. The static was terrible and we could only hear a word now and then. The voice was loud and masterful and spoke perfect English. There was reference to Germany and America and that they could no longer appeal to reason, etc. That is about all we could understand of the message. This was our first and last contact by radiotelephony. Because we did not have good reception on 92 meters, Mr. R switched back to 405 kc.

"OUR SECOND APPEASEMENT TO THE PEOPLE OF EARTH. SHORT WAVE BROADCAST. WE AWAIT, WE AWAIT. WHY BE IN SUCH—WHEN HASTE IS—. THIS MUST BE THE TIME. THIS MUST BE. HASTE, HASTE. WE CANNOT STAND BY AND SEE ANOTHER WASTE OF CREATION. THIS IS THE TIME. CANNOT FAIL. CANNOT FAIL. THIS CAN BE THE END OF ALL ON SARAS. THE LANDING WILL BE FOR SURE. SOON, SOON, HASTE.. IS ALL IN READINESS? YOU MUST BE THERE SO MUCH DEPENDS 4 K-4. 40 MILES OFF K-4."

• • •

There was a long pause before transmission began again. We couldn't understand what they meant by K-4. We thought it might refer to a certain area on a map. Would this mean they had changed their mind in regard to the chosen landing site? Mr. R finally asked them what K-4 was.

• • •

"SORRY NOW YOU MUST KNOW. K-4 SPACE SHIP

105

OUTSIDE. THIS MUST BE A DANGER SIGN TO THE WON-
DER OF EARTH PEOPLES. THE LANDING WILL BE FOR
SURE. WE DON'T CARE IF WE ARE SEEN BUT MUST BE
ON THE WATCH, BE CAREFUL. WILL BE THERE IF NO
OUTSIDE—. FROM MASAR."

This does not seem to be a very long contact, but
there may be many pauses before a complete message is
received. The code itself is a wonderful thing to hear. The
quality is very unusual and the speed of transmission is
very fast. It was necessary for Mr. R to request that they
transmit slower if possible. They then sent about three
words at a time, but the speed itself was in no way
reduced. Perhaps, because of the nature of their sending
device, they cannot slow down the transmission notice-
ably. Always, just before a message would come in, a loud
signal would be sent. This was used to alert Mr. R so that
he could get back to his set before the code began.

All of us had been trying to decide about Mr. R's
father-in-law. The old gentleman thought we were going
on a picnic the following day. Several of the women were
helping Mrs. R in her kitchen prepare chicken, sand-
wiches, etc. Mrs. R didn't know what to do with her father.
If she took him to the landing site, he might prevent the
landing by his presence. Also, because of his extremely
poor health condition, he might suffer a heart attack if he
saw a ship. On the other hand, if she left him at home, he
would be alone and would think he wasn't wanted
because he was old. She asked all of us what we thought
she should do. We could reach no final decision in the
matter. Suddenly, without Mr. R having to transmit a
word, the code came in again.

"YOU SHOULD NOT."

We believed that this was an answer to what we had
just been discussing. We thought if we did take him to the
landing site we would tell him about our radio contacts

106

and what to expect beforehand. Evidently they didn't want us to say anything to him yet. But how did they know what we had been thinking or saying. Mr. R had transmitted nothing! Did these space intelligences receive our thoughts? If we had stopped to think we would have known they did, for they contacted us by means of the "board" in the same manner. It wasn't any more unusual to do so by radio. We wanted to clear it all up, so Mr. R transmitted: "What about elder B?" Then there was a long delay of about one hour and forty-five minutes. But the message they gave us was well worth waiting for.

"WITH CARE HIS MIND SCARS STILL RESTING. TRYING AGAIN. SAW SAGAFARIS. JUPITER TRYING TO GET MIND CORRELATION OF FATHER. MIND SCARS PREVENT THEM FROM SEARCHING DEEP. CANNOT REACH FULL PROBE. MAN IS ELDERLY. TOO MUCH PROBING MAY FUSE MIND. JUPITER CANNOT REACH YOU. RELAY FROM MASAR. STILL TRYING TO REACH FULL PROBE. MIND SCARS PREVENT. THERE WILL BE FOUND SALINE SOLUTION BY BED. PLEASE CLEAN. WILL HELP CHEMICAL COMPON IN NOW THIS—DEPTH OF MIND CAN BE REACHED IN NEVER FEAR THE AGED THEY CAN HELP AGAIN WHEN THEY ARE BROUGHT TO LIFE. BODY CELL DETERIORATION NOT IN NECC A POOR CONDUCTOR. QUALITY IN WILL LET THIS GO BY TRIBUNAL ON SATURN. THEY WAIT FOR COMPLETE PROBE OF MIND. OUR K-4 MOVING AWAY FROM THE TO AWA AGFA AFFA REFIS LAQU. BETWEEN. ALL SOURCES MUST KEEP CLEAR OF ALL SPACE, THE SHIPS NUMBER 400 IN YOUR SKY. KADAR. 5555 5555 KALAR."

• • •

The space intelligences couldn't have known that Elder B was Mr. R's father-in-law, yet they said they were trying to get a mind correlation of the father! Again, they had picked up our conversation and thoughts. Also, it seemed they had seen the space craft from Sagafaris. The old gentleman was asleep all this time inside the house. They knew this fact also. He suffers from excessive, frequent passage of urine and when Mrs. R went into his bedroom to check on him, she found the solution they said would be there! It was beyond belief! How could human beings as far away as Mars and Jupiter know what was going on inside of a bedroom millions of miles away? Of course, there was a spacecraft nearby, but still many miles away. What powers these people must have! And what did they mean by, "Never fear the aged they can help again when they are brought to life?" Did this mean that these space friends had the knowledge of life and death? Could they give us proof positive of life after death? These people had the answers to man's oldest questions!

Mr. R missed much of these messages because of speed of transmission and the very nature of them. He was astounded, as we all were. He said, "If I ever doubted it, I don't now." After a long pause again, another message came in.

"MASAR TO FRIENDS OF SARAS. BE OF PEACE. MIND PROBE IS NOT INJURING HIS REACTION TO SHIP. HE WILL RECOVER IF ANY SERIOUS RESULTS DO OCCUR. HE WILL NOT IF HE IS ALL IN THE TRIBUNAL. THEY HAVE JUST MADE CONTACT WITH DEEP PROBE. CAN SEE NO HARM TO MIND. HE SHOULD BY ALL SENSE B WALK HIM TO SPOT AND IF APPEAR, TELL HIM WHAT IS EXPECTED. HE BELIEVES. IS WHAT YOU CALL IQ CAN BE GREAT DEPTH IN—HAVE IN MIND GREAT SORROW. NOT HURT KEEP HIM WARM. THIS CANNOT BE ENDING OF ALL. ENDING OF ALL. ENDING OF ALL. ENDING OF ALL. MASAR."

● ● ●

The radio contact had started about 7:30 PM and continued until late in the night. We had set up a small refracting telescope in Mr. R's backyard. While observing the moon, we were amazed to see what appeared to be a star just above its outer surface. But it was too brilliant to be a star, and it moved in a clockwise direction with the moon. We observed this object for several hours. Its movements were strange, and we wondered if this was some gigantic powerhouse of a space ship relaying our messages from Masar and Jupiter.

At last we would meet our space friends face-to-face. We could hardly believe that we were to be so honored.

September 28, 1952.

Unfortunately, our plans were poorly made. Our contacts had told us to be careful and plan wisely. None of us knew the exact landing site except Mr. R. We thought it would be safer if only one would decide and the others could follow him. Before we drove off in two cars, we told Mr. R to stop at any fork in the road where he might turn off. This would avoid separation. He did just that. He turned off the main road, parked and waited for us. But, as our car neared that point, our view was cut off by the passing of two large logging trucks from the mountains. They were traveling very fast and there was much dust. We spent the rest of the day trying to find each other. Of course, we missed the appointment for 2:00 PM. We finally found Mr. R and his car back in town about 6:00 PM. The results of this unfortunate venture made us realize that we were not prepared for such an event. We felt that we had missed the chance of a lifetime! All of our thinking at that time was directed at the landing contact as an end in itself. We have since realized that Universal service is indeed Eternal!

The goals of today become the doorways to tomorrow's duty.

We were all very hungry as Mr. R had the picnic food in his car. After eating we decided we should at least try for radio contact. We didn't think they would ever come in again. Why should they? We had failed them. Yet, we thought perhaps they would give us further instructions. A contact was made about 9:20 PM that evening.

"RADIO IS DANGEROUS. YOU MUST NOT USE YOUR RADIO. YOU WILL BE CONTACTED BY A MAN IF OUR PLANS ARE TO BE CHANGED. YES, YES. HOPE THIS SPEED IS COPY. A MAN WILL CONTACT YOU WHEN ALL IS READY. DO NOT USE RADIO. MUST HURRY. OUR TIME IS SHORT. YES YES COPY."

We waited several minutes before the next code came in.

"END. EU WE LOCATE YOU."

At 10:45 PM another message came in.

"GREETINGS, YOU HAVE—OK. DO NOT EXPUNGE YOUR MINDS. YOU HAVE INHERENT MINDS. USE THEM. WAIT."

All of these last messages were of short duration with a great pause between all of them. At 11:20 PM we again made contact.

"RADIOMAN HAS DEEP SECRET IN HIS MIND. WE WILL NOT REVEAL. WE ARE ALARMED." Mr. R turned to us and said, "If they had known about this before, they would never have picked me for your radioman." Immediately, they came in again.

"BE OF PEACE."

Again we waited several minutes.

"HAPPY. HAPPY. YOU RADIOMAN ARE INSTALLED IN THE RECORDS. GOOD. ATTENTION. SURPRISED MY

BROTHER?"

We had no idea what they meant by, "deep secret." Mr. and Mrs. R knew, however. Nevertheless, we have never been curious enough to ask them what was meant. What they were trying to convey by telling us, "installed in the records," we do not know. We received a final message at 1 :40 AM (September 29, 1952). Although much of it was a series of numbers, we copy it here for you as it was given.

"SR AGFA AWA PERI K-4 K-4 PERI AFFA AGFA ZO PERI. AGFA IS FINISHED. AGFA IS FINISHED. AGFA IS FINISHED. 110 25 AND 900 HA SO 52 AND 90 30 4 02262102 3 33 1500W 252 THE ON 1002 06000224 2257902072034."

Even though we had missed a landing with friends from other inhabited worlds, we still had a joyous time in Mr. R's "ham" shack. Anyone can imagine the suspense, the excitement that all of us felt during these radio contacts. There were usually eight or nine of us huddled together in the little shack waiting for information from our space friends! September 30, 1952 (11:00 PM):

It was a wonderful evening to look at the heavens, so we had our small telescope set up in Mr. R's backyard again. A fourteen-year-old neighbor boy came over to join us in our astronomy lesson. We were looking at Jupiter with its bands and some of its twelve moons, when this boy said that he had been having strange dreams lately. He said that a voice in his dream told him to tell no one about them, yet while he talked to us he had a strong impression to tell us. The moment he related their details we told him to go into the "ham" shack and write down everything he could remember.

This young man's name is Ronnie Tucker and he is a student in Arizona. His most amazing dream took place

111

the same night that the mind-probe was relayed from Jupiter. After the voice had warned him not to tell anyone of what he saw, he awoke from the dream covered with perspiration and looked out of his window. He said there was a beam of light about one foot wide, and tubular in shape, misty white, coming from far out in space and going directly into that part of Mr. R's home where his father-in-law was sleeping! Did young Ronnie Tucker see the beam that was conducting the mind-probe on Elder B? He must have, for he knew nothing of our research and couldn't possibly have timed the dream with the Jupiter radio message.

Mr. R wanted to tell the boy about our work, but was afraid to. He told him that there were certain things he should know, but it might take a week or so to decide in his case. The receiving set was turned on to 405 kc. while all this was going on. Immediately the following message came through, and Mr. R hadn't transmitted a thing!

"K4 K4 K4 THIS IS K4 K4 K4 THIS IS K4. OK ON THE K4 K4 OK ON THE NEW ONE. K4 K4 1."

This was truly wonderful! Our space friends accepted this boy. Now we were certain that, if they wanted to, they could know every thought, action and deed of man on Earth. Ronnie told us that in another dream they told him that they wanted to save our planet. They said they would do all they could with our help. They told him they believed that no man should destroy another, but that all men should live Universal Law and love everyone and to live in peace, working together. They assured him that life was eternal.

At 6:30 PM another "board" contact was made.

• • •

112

"This is Ankar-22 of Jupiter speaking. Jupiter is the mental research center of this Solar System. We will continue to help. On your earth there are magnetic anomalies. Your scientists wonder why meteorites fall in a pattern and in certain locations over the world. They also wonder why great civilizations are found where meteorites are found. The answer is simple. The anomalies attract the meteorites, and these same anomalies amplify Universal influx from outer space. Therefore, you will find better living conditions, finer art and music and so on in the same place you find the meteorites."

Our space friends had told us that we would be contacted by a man when all was ready. This "man" undoubtedly would be an inhabitant of another planet. We were most excited over this possibility.

During the month of September, 1952, "saucers" were being seen everywhere by competent observers. The entire world was becoming sky conscious.

During the week of October 5th a cousin of Mr. R's was visiting him in _. This man knew nothing of our research and had never mentioned "saucers" to Mr. R before. One night the two men were in the radio shack when they suddenly heard a strange low hum and a buzzing sound. Mr. R asked his cousin to go outside and see what it was. "Come here quickly," his cousin called. Mr. R arrived too late to see a strange, orange-colored, oval-shaped object hovering directly above his antenna. He said, "What do you think it was?" His cousin replied, "That was a flying saucer." At once they made an attempt to establish radio contact, but it was unsuccessful.

On October 12th at 1:00 PM an unusual thing happened. We make mention of it here because so many other people, in dealing with "saucer phenomena," have noticed the same thing. We were in Winslow at Al's house, when suddenly we smelled a very powerful, strong odor. It

113

was similar to burning metal in acid. We could not locate the source of this odor, and it seemed to be only in the house.

On October 21st at 8:10 PM, a small private plane crashed and burned at Winslow, Arizona. This plane was on a mercy flight to a Phoenix hospital with a fourteen-months-old polio victim. All four passengers were instantly killed. One of the workers at the Winslow Timber Company was working late, and saw the plane take off and minutes later burst into flames. He told the C. A. A. investigators that immediately after the crash, and before the ambulance and fire truck had arrived, an orange streak sped across the sky and apparently landed by the stricken plane. We know that the "saucers" do not harm anyone. Perhaps they knew of the child and tried to help. Of course, we do not know just what did take place.

We were now trying to separate our own thoughts from those of the space intelligences. We used the "board" rarely, for we felt it might be hindering our progress in the development of more direct telepathic contact.

November 1, 1952 (6:30 PM):
"Artok of Pluto speaking. Have no fright, all is right. Our ships are silver lights; lights of beauty; lights of duty."

"Ankar-22. Please concentrate, as we are going to go a step ahead in our telepathic work. One of you will receive a beautiful message from our brother, Ponnar. Your planet is called Saras because of the repetition of cataclysms that have visited you. Only technical advance has been made on Saras, and this is the wrong kind of achievement for you are now engulfed in darkness that has no equal."

"Itegga speaking. Men of Saras have sought only the ways of the flesh. They have a form of spirituality, but deny the power and majesty of the Creator. The so-called

114

educated man is a fool, the nations are bathed in the blood of myriads of young men, women and children. What will Saras do with her new powers? You are as children with a dangerous toy. We are out in the vastness, and we watch your industries where greed is born; your capitals where wars are born; your laboratories where discoveries are made. We see the birth cradle and we see the early death shroud. There is something far more beautiful, more satisfying, than you have attained. We have been observing you for a long time now. We are your brothers. Have we not shown this to be true over and over again? If there is violence, it will be of your making, not ours! We know that among you there are those who desire and seek the love and knowledge that alone makes man free. We have tasted of it, and it is good, it is sweet. Look up, people of Saras. Be of one mind and purpose. We are not unattainable, for we are here with you! We wait, we watch, we listen!"

• • •

Many other messages were received by members of our group by direct telepathic contact, which we never would have received had we not become as one mind. It took weeks of meditation and concentration, holding self down, and allowing ourselves to become attuned to the influx from the Universe.

The Universe has much to offer us if we but stop our senseless wars, and exploitation of our brothers, and return once more to a true realization of Creation. Wonderful and almost unbelievable things await us if we but awaken and arise to meet those who are now awakening throughout the world.

November 20, 1952:
Mr. and Mrs. Williamson with Mr. and Mrs. Bailey

115

were in company with three other people in the Desert near Desert Center, California, when a cigar-shaped mother ship was observed by all present and a personal contact was made with one of the occupants of a scout-type "saucer." This amazing account is related in full in *Flying Saucers Have Landed,* by Desmond Leslie and George Adamski.

Many things happened during December, 1952 and January, February, 1953. "Saucer" sightings increased and Nature went on a rampage. We need not go into that for the newspapers and radio broadcasts covered it thoroughly. However, there were many sightings of great importance that were never heard of by the man in the street.

On December 21, 1952, Mr. R and five other residents of Arizona, observed a large, cigar-shaped mother-craft over the city. They watched it from 5:00 PM until dark. Two smaller "saucers" were seen to enter the larger craft, and a few minutes later one left the mother-ship. This was observed through field-glasses.

On February 3, 1953, Mr. and Mrs. Williamson were coming home from town in Prescott, Arizona, when they observed two "saucers" come within a few feet of the ground. These craft were close enough so that the general outline and the light on top could be observed. There was absolutely no sound. About 10:00 PM the same night Mr. Williamson saw another "saucer" with an amber light go directly over his house. It was very low. Since this time many of these space craft have been seen in Northern Arizona and elsewhere. Many people are afraid to tell about what they have seen!

February 15, 1953 (11:25 PM):
We were at Mr. R's for a short conference. We were

116

trying to decide what we should do about this report you are now reading. How should it be written? Should all of the facts be given to the public? We did know that we should continue to be of one mind and then carefully make our plans. We knew, also, that our space friends would want the truth given. Nothing else would do!

Mr. R had the radio set turned on, as he always does when he is in the radio shack. One never knows when a signal might come in from the spacecraft intelligences. He had transmitted nothing. In fact, he doesn't need to transmit any more. They will answer any and all problems they feel important by coming in on the receiver if it is on. Mr. R also wondered if V (..._) wasn't really EU (..._)?

Suddenly a radio code signal just seemed to "slide" in on 405 kc. At first, Mr. R couldn't make any sense out of the dot and dash system. Finally, one word stood out. It was: "CENTURAS." We do not know what it could mean except it closely resembles the name of a constellation. Then a very understandable message came through.

"OK THIS TIME IS FOR YOU TO DECIDE. AR. OK OK OK THIS TIME IS FOR YOU TO DECIDE. WE CAN NOT, AK A. AFFA FROM THE P. RA RRR OK K5 K5 FROM THE PLA CHANT RRT IT."

The message ended at 12:05 AM, February 16, 1953. They would not decide for us on this report. It was up to us! So, we have given it to you exactly as it happened. It is unfortunate that some of the messages were not understandable. Affa was on a ship called K-5, and he was apparently going to give us the name of his own planet and the ship's origin.

We know that all radios in the world are not silent. Many of them are now receiving information from our brothers in the sky! We hope that this report will awaken interest amongst others, and that they will honestly attempt contact with our visitors from space. They have come a long way to help us. Let us extend to them the hand of friendship and welcome!

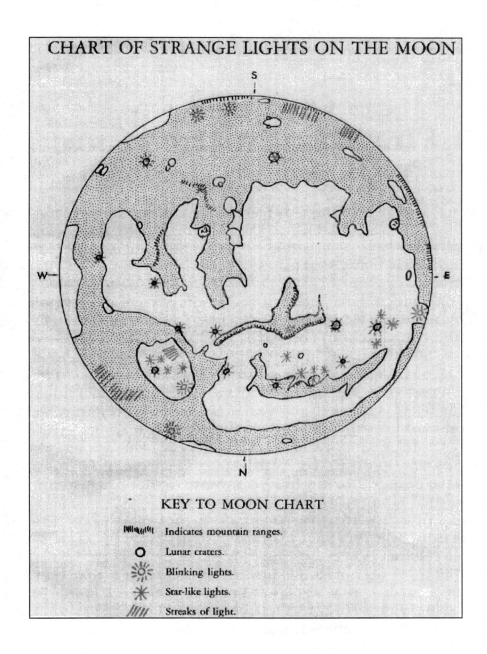

CHART OF STRANGE LIGHTS ON THE MOON

KEY TO MOON CHART

Indicates mountain ranges.	
Lunar craters.	
Blinking lights.	
Star-like lights.	
Streaks of light.	

Chapter 8
The Man in the Moon

Men of other worlds have beaten us to our own satellite, and have established bases there. This is the reason why we have seen strange lights and blinkings on the moon for many years now. These have never been adequately explained.

Strange lights, etc., on the moon have been reported by reputable astronomers over a long period of time. The following has been observed:

Star-like lights in the Crater Aristarchus; a pyramid in the open space of Linne; an "X" visible in the Crater Eratosthenes; a strange symbol visible in the Crater Plinus; the letter Gamma in the Crater Littrow; a luminous cable drawn across the Crater Eudoxus in the Northwest Quadrant of the Moon; strange happenings in the Crater Proclus, and in the Crater Picard. Many strange illuminations have been sighted in the Northwest Quarter or Quadrant of the Moon.

At a distance, the space craft do look like "stars." The reason: They operate in a magnetic field just the same as all celestial bodies do! How long they have been on the Moon we do not know, but we can be certain that they have used it as a base ever since they began coming to Earth. We have not had telescopes very long, but as soon as this instrument was utilized we saw strange things on our satellite! The "man in the moon" made us laugh once, but he's an actuality after all!

Mr. Tom Comella, Jr., young astronomer of Cleveland, Ohio, has been kind enough to furnish us with a moon chart of lights sighted there.

For several months now, we have been receiving letters from all over the United States, Canada, Mexico, England and other countries. Many of these have been from scientific groups and individuals. Several well-known astronomers have told us in writing that they firmly believe the saucer phenomena to be interplanetary in origin. We have these letters on file.

Chapter 9
Saucers Still Speaking

Many groups are now experimenting in radio, trying to contact the "saucers." Some of these groups have had success. Others have received nothing and others have not received anything from the "saucers" themselves over their radio receivers, but "saucer" sightings have coincided with their transmissions.

We have had more personal contact recently with the "saucers," but this is of such a nature, that we cannot put it into print just now.

One group, working with radio communication in Ohio, has had success in contacting the "discs." We have been in touch with them by letter.

Mr. Lonzo Dove of Broadway, Virginia writes the following: "You asked me to describe the strange speech that came over my FM radio set. My wife and I heard it the first time, but a whole crowd of us heard it the last time, and special effort was made to get some intelligible word out of the conversation which seemed to be between a man and a woman. The first time I found the signal at 98 mc. on April 15, 1952. It was repeated the next day at the same time: 4:15 to 5 :25 PM EST. The signal was very powerful, as indicated by the electric eye, but the voices were low in volume, as if our radio receivers were not precisely designed for the type of modulation being used. The sounds were of even tone like chanting, as if two trumpets were speaking, one low pitch and the other high pitch, like a man and a woman.

"But the sounds were divided into words and sentences, one, then the other speaking. There wasn't a single word in English. On April 16, 1952, I photographed a huge cloud circle in the sky of this region. It was not caused by jet vapor trails. That same night the enormous vapor trails over Alaska caused the military alert, and the communication line between Alaska and the United States went dead. Also that same day, astronomers observed a double cloud on Mars that rose nearly 100 miles above the surface of the planet. Nothing like it has ever been seen before!

"The next radio voice came on March 16, 1953. It was the same chanting speech, but one of our listeners said he heard the word: 'Washington.' This was the only understandable word. Of course, this word would be the same no matter where used. I think this was on 103 mc. Unfortunately, I have mislaid my notes. It was also in the evening. I made some tests this time, and found the signal came from a certain direction, straight to the radio, NOT through the aerial. When I stood or placed my hand in a certain place, the signal would dim and static would come in. Evidently this message just happened to affect the FM set on that particular frequency."

You may have had an experience similar to Mr. Dove's. If you have, please let us know about it. Mr. Dove is an excellent photographer, and is well-known for his work in physics and astronomy. He has been very active in saucer investigation for several years now.

On January 29, 1950 in the country of Spain, several radio owners reported strange speech reception, while saucers were being observed flying over the country. This was just about a month before the Great Saucer Armada

arrival over Farmington, New Mexico. Other saucer sightings were seen at this time. It will be remembered that
most of our own communication was done in the months
when saucers were being seen everywhere.

In Iowa there's a very fine group working with radio.
This group includes prominent professional men and several radio operators. On March 18, 1953 (this almost came
on the March 16, 1953 date of Mr. Dove' observations) the
following happened to one of the members of this group.

"I was driving from, Iowa westward. It was about
12:45 AM, I noticed that on 550 kc. on the radio a very
strong code sending was going on. It was a very foggy
night and raining. The code became very loud and then
would fade away at intervals. I stopped at the top of several high hills to see if I could see anything, but no luck.
Finally at one point the fog thinned out, and I saw a huge
round glow coming down through the fog towards me. It
became larger and larger with a bluish-purple color. Suddenly the fog broke away and to the east of the road I was
standing on, there shone a bright red light, then it turned
to white, then back to red again. After changing several
times, the fog closed in again and the light appeared as
the purplish glow once more. I felt I was being watched! I
drove on to—, Iowa after the fog became thicker. The code
sending continued and seemed to follow me all the way to
town. I dug my partner out of bed at 2:30 AM and at his
house among large trees, the purplish glow came down
through the fog again as my partner and his wife watched.
The code signals kept coming in very strong for an hour,
finally faded some, so we went to bed at 4:00 AM still able
to hear the signals, however."

Several times immediately after, this group would try
radio communications, members would sight "flying
saucers" over their town. And since they have been in
contact via radio, many sightings have been made in that

part of Iowa. One time in their messages there was mention of a Bible passage and another time they received: "WE FIND FEW NOW READY!" This speaks for itself!

Some groups have proven the telepathy part of the radio experiment by receiving messages pertaining to something they had never transmitted to the "discs."

Sightings are still being made all over the world, but there seems to be a lull at this time compared to sightings made in the fall of other years when usually there is a great deal of activity.

However, the "saucers" are still here and have very important plans for earth. There will be more catastrophe in the future. The Ionian Island disaster by earthquake off Greece recently is very significant. Our fault lines are under great stress and are giving at certain points. Those Islands are directly over the area where three main, very large fault lines converge! Also, about that time, an enormous exploding light was viewed in Denmark.

Yes, the Saucers Are Still Speaking! Let's listen to what they have to say!

Epilogue

"Yet so shall it be; these fruitless strifes, these ruinous wars shall pass away, and the Most Great Peace shall come."—Baha'u'llah.

As we complete this report, we watch the newspaper headlines and listen to the newscasts with great interest:

"Fantastic Sky 'Spook' Sighted Over Dallas; Navy Gives Chase" (*San Diego Evening Tribune,* Jan. 6, 1953).

"U. S. Jets Chase Saucers Toward Siberia—Radar Picks Up 'Saucers' Over Japan; Pursuit Fails." (*Los Angeles Examiner,* Jan. 22, 1953).

"Weird Lights Fly Near Kurile Isles—Air Force Reports Observations By Pilots, Radar Over North Japan." (*The Phoenix Gazette*, Jan. 21, 1953).

"Pilot Sees 'Disk' Make Pass At Jet." (*The Phoenix Gazette,* Jan. 27, 1953) .

"Jet Chases 'Saucer' At Beach." (*Los Angeles Examiner,* Jan. 30, 1953) .

"Marine Flier Chases Disk Over Southland—Jet Fighter Unable to Overtake Object; Four Others Reported." (*Los Angeles Times,* Jan. 30, 1953).

"Pilot Sights 'Saucers'; Fiery Disc Races Jet." (*Phoenix Gazette,* Jan. 30, 1953).

We could go on and on with newspaper stories and the reports of fearless commentators. The predictions made by our friendly communicators are coming true daily. They have told us that we would see more and more

126

of them in the near future. They said they couldn't stand by and see another waste. Many of the people of Earth shall see them and no longer doubt who or what they are. They come as our friends to aid us in a dark hour on this planet. Soon, we believe they may even land in great numbers. But this is not an invasion of our world. Billions of earths were created for mankind. They need not take any one of them by aggressive action.

Let us look up and watch our skies, for our atomic blasts have alerted the Universe, and the "flying saucers" are here to stay! There are those who hope they will go away, but they never will!

For centuries scientists have set up theories which are guesses based on carefully observed facts. When a few of these scientists want to leave the Desert of Past Mistakes and Guesses, they are held back by the Giant known as Orthodox Science. This Giant has many followers, who claim him to be "All Perfection." In the 15th century his mighty voice rang out to men like Columbus, "Thou shalt not believe the earth is round!" Today he stands there still, shouting, "Thou shalt not see nor believe in 'flying saucers."

There are many well-known scientists today who are devoted "slaves" of this Giant. They are presumably dedicated to bringing the light to all mankind, yet they hold aloft their own puny torch, hoping someone will carry it on. But its light is dim and flickering. Soon a greater light shall take its place. While the Giant gleefully watches in the darkness, others slip past him into a new day of greater knowledge.

The renowned astrophysicist, Dr. Donald H. Menzel, of Harvard Observatory, has written a book that is supposed to tell the "whole truth and nothing but the truth" about "flying saucers." Other scientists have said his laboratory experiments cannot be duplicated in nature. University students who flock to his lectures come away very disappointed. They say, "We couldn't help but feel that Dr. Menzel was covering up and leaving something out. It's that 'something' that has us worried!"

While Menzel was playing with his car headlights, another world famous astronomer, Dr. Clyde Tombaugh, discoverer of the planet Pluto, was seeing a spaceship! In the sky over Las Cruces, New Mexico, in the summer of 1948, whizzing silently overhead from south to north, was an oval-shaped object. It had about a dozen windows which were clearly visible at the front and along the side. The rear trailed off into a "shapeless luminescence." It was traveling too fast for a plane and too slow for a meteor. Many have said that no astronomer of repute has reported seeing "unidentified aerial phenomena." However, as we can see from Dr. Tombaugh's report, they are wrong in their statements.

Other so-called "authorities" were seeing swarms of giant locusts crossing the moon. The same "authorities" claimed the moon was without atmosphere! Locusts in a vacuum! While they were seeing reflected light on floating dandelion seeds; spiders riding gossamer wisps in the sun's eye; "fliting flies"; and extraterrestrial flying barnyards; other scientists with vision, who are also "men of science," were seeing the "saucers" as they really are—spacecraft!

Even stodgy *Harper's* Magazine succumbed to commercialism. They enticed their readers into buying a recent issue by placing the title, "Little Men and Flying Saucers," on the cover page. The article, by Dr. Loren C. Eiseley, professor of anthropology at the University of Pennsylvania, drags the reader through tales of mermaids, griffins, salamandrine beasts of the coal swamps, carnival freaks, and Darwinism. Very little, if anything, is said about the "flying saucers." For a man who is presumably a trained observer, this is indeed a poor observation. He tries to bring in material that has no bearing on the "saucer" phenomena in order to disprove it. Why? Because he and his cohort, the Giant, have said, "Thou shalt not!"

He tells us that it is just conceivable that there may be nowhere in space a mind superior to our own! According to him the human ego likes to believe that other worlds are inhabited. And since he is so fortunate in knowing what the truth is, he tells us that man is a solitary and peculiar development on the planet Earth! While others are going forward, he is still back in the middle of the desert with Charles Darwin.

Is it egotistical to believe that men are to be found everywhere in the Universe? Or is it egotistical to believe that only the Earth is inhabited—thus making the Earth unique? Does man want to be alone on this globe with his many wars, crimes and waste? If he contemplates other inhabited worlds for a moment he sees visions of greater Powers that he may have to answer to.

Some scientists claim that the statistical probability of the life on this planet being duplicated on an other planet is so small as to be meaningless. Yet, the law of averages tells us differently! Dr. Harold C. Urey, Nobel prize winning atomic scientist, tells us that one quadrillion worlds may originate and sustain life. If we think in terms of Infinity there must be many, many more also!

Certain "authorities" accept the idea that cellular life may exist out yonder in the dark. But high or low in nature, they do not believe it will wear the shape of man. These same men tell us we are the only thinking mammals on the planet, perhaps the only thinking animals in the entire sidereal Universe. My, my, the burden of consciousness has certainly grown heavy upon us, and it is thus we torture ourselves! These men are all alone in the

Creation with their super-brains!

Anyone really studying and knowing animal life would never say that we are "the only thinking mammals on the planet."

Getting back to *Harper's* contribution to "saucer" research again, we find the article tells us that those who describe a two-foot tall men forget that a normal human brain cannot function with a capacity, at the very minimum, of less than about 900 cubic centimeters of capacity. We say that the author of this article has forgotten it is a relative matter! He mentions "meteors whispering greenly overhead." There are scientists today who would tell him that meteors are never green!

We are told that nowhere in all space or on a thousand worlds will there be men to share our loneliness. So, there may be boneless, watery, pulpy masses, but of men elsewhere, and beyond, there will be none forever!

The great scientists of Columbus' time told him that horrible monsters would swallow him and his little ships. Others are telling us the same thing today—that there may be monsters in outer space, but no men! Remember, Columbus found only more men—so will we!

Scientists who really want to leave this dry desert will do just that. All others can stay behind tortured by their terrific burden of a "super-brain" and their loneliness.

We are told Dr. Eiseley has been wandering around getting himself covered with sand burs and other prickly seeds, all of this activity being pertinent to the writing of a book. The "prickly seeds" must have gotten in his eyes, for if they had been airborne he might have seen a "flying saucer." He claims he would rather have lunch with a purple polyp than with a man from Mars. Perhaps he will get his wish!

There is still another type of Giant worshipper that uses the cloak of "spirituality" and "religion." Orthodox science or orthodox religion is the same thing. They are both demanding and dogmatic. This type of man is usually uneducated, for if he were educated he would probably be a "super-scientist." Instead, he has no choice but to be a "super-religionist." A man-made evangelist bringing "hell-fire" and "damnation" to all "sinners." This type is extremely egotistical and dogmatic.

One of these is Mr. William C. Lamb of Wyoming. He claims he has photographs of God and the Holy City. He quotes reams of Scripture to "prove" his own opinions. Yet, he believes that atomic energy was a "gift of God" to his "angelic earth children" so that they might blow up all the devils and imps, sending them to everlasting "fire and brimstone." This type does not realize that God cannot be photographed. (Even their Bible will tell them so.) The Creator is the unmeasured and timeless one!

We do not believe that a loving God would give man a "gift" whereby he could destroy innocent women and children in a horrible holocaust! Our Mr. Lamb has astronomical photographs of the Orion Nebula. (Interpreted by him, of course.) God's Throne is supposed to be there. He is telling us that the Creator is smaller and more insignificant than His own Creation! He says the Omnipotence and Omniscience of Deity is a secret that no man is able to fathom, yet he claims to know more about the "flying saucers" than anyone else. He is contradictory and fortunately this type is easily discerned. There isn't enough intelligence amongst them to dupe us with lengthy scientific language.

To all of this, we say what Charles Fort said, "The trash that is clogging an epoch must be cleared away!"

We see a vision of the future. A world without a slave, men at last free, where our loyalty is not to something called "mine," but to all humanity, to the ideal of a higher Universal civilization which will spew out war forever as

131

the vilest of all human defilements. There wilt be no imaginary boundary lines of nationality, race, color or creed. The Earth will be swept clean of these false walls that for centuries have shut man from man, nation from nation, and have filled the earth with lamentation and tears, with rivalry and hate, cruelty and oppression, injustice and greed, selfishness and pride, bloodshed, battlefields, and death.

It will be a new world where work and worth go hand in hand, where men's lips are rich with love and truth. A race will exist without disease of flesh or brain, for health will come to all as a divine heritage. And above it all will be the Eternal Father.

Those who cling to the old methods and beliefs will go down with the old order. This is the uncovering period. Soon man will feel deeply that he is indeed his brother's keeper!

Our only remedy for saving ourselves is to turn from hate and national enmity to love and a realization of the Fatherhood of God, the Motherhood of Nature, and the Brotherhood of Man.

Appendix

We would like to let you know what some of the world's experts are saying.

Brig. Gen. Ernest Moore, former Chief, Air Force Intelligence:

"First off, the Russians have nothing to do with these so-called 'saucers.' I'll swear to that on a stack of Bibles, if you like. Second, we don't have any secret new types of aircraft that could have started all this commotion."

The theory that the saucers were hostile aircraft was carefully studied and rejected. As one scientist said, "The performances of these 'saucers' not only surpass the development of present science but the development of present fiction-science writers."

As of August 25, 1952, Captain Ruppelt, Air Force, said more competent observers than ever before have been reporting "saucers." The Captain, who started as a one-man agency, now has eight full-time assistants. The Air Force is buying a hundred special cameras, which it hopes will help determine what the objects are made of, and it is considering buying several photographic telescopes of a new type, costing as much as five thousand dollars a piece, with which a continuous photographic record can be made nightly of the sky over the whole hemisphere. After several years and nearly two thousand reported sightings of a serious nature, there is no discussion in Air Force circles of abandoning the pursuit of the elusive "saucers."

Twenty-five per cent of the observers interrogated by the Aerial Phenomena Officer in the last few years have been military pilots. Eight per cent have been commercial pilots, some with as much as twenty years' experience in the air, and at one stage in the current phase of the investigation, even a few physicists at Los Alamos, New Mexico, men who make a fetish of objectivity, were interviewed after they reported having seen puzzling lights hovering above their atomic energy laboratories.

On July 21, 1952, Senior Air Traffic Controller for the Civil Aeronautics Administration at the National Airport's Air Route Traffic Control Center, in Washington, D. C., informed the Air Force, and the public that early that morning his radarscope had picked up ten unidentifiable objects flying over various parts of the capital, including the prohibited area around the White House. Controller Harry G. Barnes said, "There is no other conclusion I can reach but that for six hours on the morning of the twentieth of July there were at least ten unidentifiable objects moving above Washington. They were not ordinary aircraft. Nor in my opinion could any natural phenomena account for these spots on our radar. Neither shooting stars, electrical disturbances, nor clouds could, either. Exactly what they are, I don't know. Now you know as much about them as I do. And your guess is as good as mine."

On August 6, 1952, an Army physicist at Fort Belvoir, Virginia, created an effect similar to "flying saucers" in his laboratory by introducing molecules of ionized air into a partial vacuum in a bell jar, and three days later an internationally known authority on atmospheric conditions said of the physicist's experiment, "I know of no conditions of the earth's atmosphere, high or low, which would duplicate those needed to make the laboratory models."

134

Dr. Fitts and other Project Saucer scientists, said, "Some of the sightings might be blamed on muscat volitantes ("flitting flies"), the medical term for small solid particles that float about in the field of the eye, casting a shadow on the retina and moving as the eye moves."

Dr. George Valley, a nuclear physicist at the Massachusetts Institute of Technology; staff members of the research firm of Hand Corporation; an assortment of physicists and aerodynamicists who specialize in the study of the stratosphere and the space beyond it; and the electronics experts attached to the Cambridge Field Station were all searching for physical rather than psychological explanations, and some fairly strange theories occurred to them— the possibility that extraterrestrial animals were flying into our atmosphere, for example. However, no data turned up to support the arresting idea!

The astronomers concluded that the atmosphere of Venus was composed largely of carbon dioxide and immense, opaque clouds of formaldehyde droplets, and this precluded the practice of astronomy, and hence the concept of a Universe and the idea of spaceships.

We feel that perhaps the people of Venus would develop better telescopes than we because of the above conditions, and would therefore have finer equipment than we for viewing the heavens. That cloud-layer might excite their curiosity to find out what was beyond it !

There are other theories about Venus, however John Robinson in "The Universe We Live In," tells us that the dust-bowl theory is based on the spectroscopic examination of the upper atmosphere of Venus which reveals no water-vapor and quantities of carbon-monoxide at that level. He points out that at 70 miles above the surface of the Earth the atmosphere contains no oxygen or water vapor at all, and that the atmosphere is almost 100% hydrogen, an entirely unbreathable and highly inflammable gas. The Earth nevertheless teems with life despite the fact that there is no oxygen or water vapor in the outer 400 miles of its atmosphere. All oxygen, water vapor, and hence life exist only within a few miles of the surface. This man is not afraid to come to grips with the most modern theories and he searchingly analyzes them.

Months ago our space friends told us that the moon had an atmosphere. The other day, Dr. Harlow Shapley, astronomer at Harvard College Observatory, announced that the moon does indeed, have an atmosphere!

Fred Hoyle, British astronomer, says, "I think that all our present guesses are likely to prove but a very pale shadow of the real thing."

Dr. Lincoln La Paz, University of New Mexico, claims that the "saucers" are not meteors, because they do not look like meteors. He says that the "fireballs" are not shooting stars or meteorites, because meteorites glow for only short periods and invariably make loud noises, while the "fireballs" and "saucers" are silent. These objects, he says, can reverse direction and cruise back and forth, travel at high speeds in wide, sweeping circles, are spherical or disc-shaped, give off a steady yellow light for the most part, and travel at extremely high altitudes. Also, meteors are rarely green in color.

The "saucers" are not balloons. Mr. J. J. C. Kaliszewski, a supervisor of balloon manufacture, says, "The 'saucers' are strange, terrifically fast. They have a peculiar glow. One seemed to have a halo around it, with a dark under-surface. We see no vapor trail."

Dr. Albert Einstein on July 23, 1952, said, "Those people have seen something. What it is I do not know and I am not curious to know."

Father Francis J. Connell, C.Sc.R., Dean of the Catholic University's School of Sacred Theology said, "It is well for Catholics to know that the principles of their faith are entirely reconcilable with even the most astounding possibilities regarding life on other planets....Theologians have never dared to limit the omnipotence of God to the creation of the world we know." He added, "If these supposed rational beings should possess the immortality of body once enjoyed by Adam and Eve, it would be foolish for our superjet or rocket pilots to try to shoot them. They would be unkillable."

Anatol J. Schneider, seismologist, stated on June 10th, 1946, in San Francisco, California, that there was great danger of cracking the Earth's surface with atomic bombing by great danger of climate changes occurring throughout the world. It was the underwater bombing that was to be the most feared.

The hands of the clock on the cover of the Bulletin of the Atomic Scientists now stand at three minutes to midnight. When the Bulletin began, the cover pictured a clock with the hands at eight minutes to midnight. The hands are moving up! The hands reflect the feeling of many scientists that since 1945 the world has moved closer to the catastrophe of atomic warfare—that it has become increasingly urgent that we find a solution to the problem of the peaceful utilization of the work of science for the benefit of all mankind.

The world is now close to the Midnight Hour!

Glossary

ACTAR...From Mercury; Radio Center of our Solar System.

ADEE...Capital City of Etonya; Jupiter.

ADU...From Hatonn in Andromeda.

AGFA AFFA...From Uranus.

ANKAR-22...From Jupiter.

ARTOK...From Pluto

AWA...A contact.

BARRAGA...Means friends in the Solex Mal.

BELGA...Um's special space craft.

BELL FLIGHT..."Flying Saucer" Fleet.

BEN...Means good in the Solex Mal.

CHAN...The Planet Earth; means "afflicted" in certain ancient languages.

CLACTEEM...Special ship from Masar for landing contacts.

CREATIVE SPIRIT...God; the Creator.

CRYSTAL BELL...A "flying saucer."

DA...Code for Outer Space Contact.

DEIMOS...One of the artificial satellites of Mars.

ELALA...Planet 15 of Solar System 22; formerly called Wogog.

ELEX...Young son of Zo and Um.

ETONYA...The Planet Jupiter.

EU...Code symbol for the Planet Earth.

FOWSER...The "dark moon," or second moon of

138

Earth.

GARR...From Pluto.

GIN-GWIN...Chippewa Indian word for "flying saucer."

HATONN...A planet in the galactic system of Andromeda.

KADAR LACU...Kalar Laqu: Head of the Universal Tribunal on Saturn.

KARAS...A contact.

K-4...A space ship.

K-5...A space ship.

LOMEC...From Venus.

MACAS...Neptunian cattle.

MASAR...The Planet Mars.

MORNING STAR...The Planet Venus.

NAH-9...Head of Solar X Group; a contact group from the Planet Neptune.

NORO...Head of a landing contact group.

OARA...Planetary representative of Saturn.

ORION...Universal evil influence emanates from this area in the heavens.

PATRAS...Planet next beyond Pluto in our own Solar System which contains twelve planets altogether.

PHOBOS...One of the artificial satellites of Mars.

PLANET 5...Formerly the planet between Mars and Jupiter, now known as the asteroid belt (Lucifer).

PONNAR...A Universal Head from the Planet Hatonn.

REGGA...Planetary representative of Mars.

RO...From the Toresoton Solar System.

R-3...A space ship.

SAFANIAN...Another Solar System.

SAGAFARIS...Another Solar System.

SARAS...The Planet Earth; in ancient Chaldean it means "repetition." (Also, Saros).

SEDAT...Keeper of Records in the Temple of Records

on Hatonn.

SOLAR SYSTEM-22...Another Solar System containing 22 planets.

SOLAS...The Sun.

SOLEX MAL...The original language once spoken on Earth; the mother-tongue; the Solar-tongue; spoken by all people of Outer Space; a symbolic, pictographic language.

SUTTKU...Judge of the Saturn Council.

TERRA...From the Planet Venus; on Ship-49.

TIME-KEEPERS...A group that computes Cycles.

TONAS...Musical instruments.

TORESOTON...Another Solar System.

TOUKA...From Pluto.

TROCTON...A space ship of the Solar X Group.

UM...From Mars; wife of Zo.

VEC...Means space in the Solex Mal.

WAN-4...Representative of the Safanian Solar System.

ZAGO...A member of a contact group; from Mars.

ZO...Strom Neptune; Head of a Masar contact group.

Afterword

(With Special Thanks to Donald Ware)

In the time since Williamson's original words were put down, naturally much has happened to add to his research. The number of messages being beamed to Earth seems to be ever increasing, and the seriousness of the situation certainly has not diminished.

The truth is that the "source" of these broadcasts have seemingly stepped up their campaign to get the word across to us. Not only do they continue to utilize radio, but they have modernized themselves in that mysterious TV broadcasts and weird video "malfunctions" have now taken us over.

Recently we received a rather lengthy investigative report about this matter from engineer Donald Ware of Fort Walton Beach, Florida. Ware has been probing deeply into the voice phenomenon for some time and has dubbed such transmissions "Instrumented Trans-Communications" or ITCs.

In order to "wrap up" our dialogue, we hereby conclude these pages with Ware's findings...which are just as mind blowing as anything presented elsewhere in this book.

$$\bullet \ \bullet \ \bullet$$

INSTRUMENTED TRANS-COMMUNICATION (ITC): In the UFO literature, I occasionally find a case where a telephone, a tape recorder, radio or television is apparently used by a higher intelligence to send a message to humans. The Spring 1993 issue of the Institute of Noetic Sciences (IONS) *Quarterly Review* had an interesting article titled, "When Dimensions Cross." Research groups have studied this phenomenon for years. For example, after 25 years of research, Swedish film producer, Friedrich Juergenson, published his findings in the 1964 book *Voices from the Universe.* Even after his death in 1987, Juergenson continued to work from the "spiritside" with other ITC researchers on the "earthside." His face appeared on a television screen during these research sessions.

A Luxembourg research group contacted a voice on the radio called TECHNICIAN. The IONS *Quarterly Review* article by Willis Harman concludes by saying:

"While the declared spiritside aim of ITC is eventually to be able to circumvent the experiencers' psyche altogether, what is in practice today appears to be a telepathically assisted instrumental communication. It appears that researchers' beliefs, thoughts and attitudes affect ITC contacts, but to a lesser degree than during the phenomenon of 'channeling.' From the technical point of view, then, the ultimate aim of ITC is to develop an electronic system that will work independently of the psyches of the earthside participants, and the Luxembourg team seems to be getting close.

"What do the 'higher beings' hope to accomplish with ITC? According to TECHNICIAN, they want everyone to know that life continues beyond physical death. For many people today, faith in age-old religious texts is not enough; they need solid evidence of an afterlife, which ITC may provide."

Another example of a television apparently being used by a higher intelligence was captured accidentally(?) on December 23, 1990, when a lady in New Jersey was photographing her son. He was playing near a television that was not turned on. A clear picture of an alien head with large, dark eyes and a circular indentation, high on the side of the head, was investigated by the New Jersey MUFON group. Their report was finally published in MUFON's *New Jersey Chronicle* of September–December, 1992.

I find it significant that the alien head looked very much like the head of the alien on the back of the AMOCO ad that first appeared in aerospace magazines, shortly before this event.

11